DATE DUE			

DISCARDED

D1127042

HISTORICAL STATISTICS OF THE UNITED STATES, 1790-1970
Vol. II - The Midwest

HISTORICAL STATISTICS OF THE UNITED STATES 1790-1970
Vol. I — The South
Vol. II — The Midwest
In Preparation:
Vol. III — The Northeast
Vol. IV — The West

HISTORICAL STATISTICS OF THE UNITED STATES, 1790-1970

Vol. II - The Midwest

A Compilation of State-level Census Statistics for the Twelve States of

Illinois	Missouri
Indiana	Nebraska
Iowa	North Dakota
Kansas	Ohio
Michigan	South Dakota
Minnesota	Wisconsin

by

Donald B. Dodd

and

Wynelle S. Dodd

The University of Alabama Press

University, Alabama

Library of Congress Cataloging in Publication Data

Dodd, Donald B.
   Historical Statistics of the United States, 1790-1970
   Includes bibliographical references.
   CONTENTS: [v. 1] Historical Statistics of the
South, 1790-1970. —v. 2. The Midwest.
   1. United States—Statistics—Collected works.
I. Dodd, Wynelle S., joint author. II. Title.
HA215.D6   317.3   75-23482
ISBN 0-8173-9701-9

TABLE OF CONTENTS

PREFACE

Historical Statistics of the Midwest resulted from repeated frustration in dealing with several aspects of census research which include: the sparsity of complete sets of census materials, the time involved in compiling workable statistics for a number of consecutive enumerations, and the difficulty in identifying the nature of statistics due to changing definitions. To counter some of these problems, the authors compiled state-level census data available for a significant number of consecutive decades and listed these items by years under the individual states. Hopefully this state-level data will help fill the statistical gap between national data in *Historical Statistics of the United States: Colonial Times to 1957* and county-level data in the computer tapes of the Inter-University Consortium for Political Research.

Historical Statistics of the Midwest is Volume II of a projected four-volume series. Volume I was *Historical Statistics of the South* (University, Alabama: The University of Alabama Press, 1973). A second edition of Volume I (compatible in content to Volume II) is in press. The remaining two volumes will provide data for the West (including Alaska and Hawaii) and the East.

Explanations of terms are in the Glossary of Terms. Footnotes relate to the source of the information. Items which relate to per cent of a total (Items 4, 35, 37, 39, 41, and 43 of the General Population, Agriculture, and Manufacturing Statistics, 1790-1970) refer to the individual state's percentage of the national total.

No attempt to draw inferences from the data has been made. However, the data have potential for correlative and inferential statistics. An example of one use of the data in this publication (and other Census data) is in *Historical Atlas of Alabama* (University, Alabama: The University of Alabama Press, 1974).

Individuals who were helpful to the authors in compiling this book include: Mrs. Jessie Cobb, Mr. Al Craig, Mrs. Frances Macon, Mrs. Annie Lee Mills, and Mrs. Frances Clark of the staff of Alabama Archives and History; Mr. Richard Pastorett and Mrs. Barbara Dekle, Auburn University at Montgomery Library; and Mr. Richard Jensen, Newberry Library, Chicago, Illinois. The U.S. Bureau of the Census also assisted by expediting the delivery of appropriate schedules of the 1970 Census.

Several people assisted in the proofreading of the original statistical tables and the galley proofs. They include Linda and Susan Dodd, Sandra Dodd, and Auburn University at Montgomery students John Eagerton, Charles Ford, Rhonda Gaskin, Joanna Hesseltine, Donna Palmer, Gary Reeves, Jane Wright, and Cecil Yawn.

Due to the complexity of the changes in the census enumerations during the past 180 years, as well as the bulk of statistical materials, there probably will be errors. Subsequent editions will correct errors noted by readers and incorporate helpful suggestions. Recommendations and comments should be sent to the authors in care of:

The University of Alabama Press
Drawer 2877
University, Alabama 35486

HISTORICAL STATISTICS OF THE UNITED STATES, 1790-1970
Vol. II - The Midwest

General Population, Agriculture, and Manufacturing Statistics, 1790-1970

ILLINOIS

Item No.	1790 (or 1789)	1800	1810	1820	1830	1840	1850	1860	1870
1. Population[1]	...	...	12,282[a]	55,211	157,445	476,183	851,470	1,711,951	2,539,891
2. Decennial rates of increase in population over preceding census[2]	...	...	...	349.5	185.2	202.4	78.8	101.1	48.4
3. Increase in population over previous census[1,3]	...	...	12,282	42,929	102,234	318,738	375,287	860,481	827,940
4. Percent distribution of population[4]	...	...	0.2	0.6	1.2	2.8	3.7	5.4	6.6
5. Population per square mile of land area[5,6]	...	...	...	...	...	...	15.2	30.6	45.4
6. Membership of House of Representatives at each apportionment[7]	...	...	1	1	3	7	9	14	19
7. White population[8,9,10]	...	...	11,501	53,837	155,061	472,254	846,034	1,704,291	2,511,096
8. Percentage increase in white population over preceding census[9,10,11]	...	...	...	368.1	188.0	204.6	79.1	101.4	47.3
9. Negro population[8,9,10]	...	...	781	1,374	2,384	3,929	5,436	7,628	28,762
10. Percentage increase in Negro population over preceding census[9,10,11,12,13,14]	...	...	...	75.9	73.5	64.8	38.4	40.3	277.1
11. Percent Negro in total population[1,8,9,10,14,15]	...	...	6.4	2.5	1.5	0.8	0.6	0.5	1.1
12. Number of slaves in the area enumerated in 1790 and in the added area[16]	...	107[b]	168	917	747	331	...	...	...
13. Urban population[17]	...	...	...	...	...	9,607	64,427	245,545	596,042
14. Percent urban increase over preceding census[17]	...	...	...	...	...	...	570.6	281.1	142.7
15. Rural population[17]	...	...	12,282	55,211	157,445	466,576	787,043	1,466,406	1,943,849
16. Percent rural increase over preceding census[17]	...	...	...	349.5	185.2	196.3	68.7	86.3	32.6
17. Percent of urban to total population[17]	...	...	...	...	...	2.0	7.6	14.3	23.5
18. Percent of rural to total population[17]	...	...	100.0	100.0	100.0	98.0	92.4	85.7	76.5
19. Number of farms[18,19]	...	...	...	...	...	...	76,208	143,310	202,803
20. Acres in farms[18,19]	...	...	...	...	...	...	12,037,412	20,911,989	25,882,861
21. Acres improved land in farms[20]	...	...	...	...	...	...	5,039,545	13,096,374	19,329,952
22. Cropland harvested, acres[18,19]	...	...	...	...	...	...	NA	NA	NA
23. Percentage increase in number of farms[18,19]	...	...	...	...	...	...	...	88.1	41.5
24. Percentage increase of land in farms[18,19]	...	...	...	...	...	...	...	73.7	23.8
25. Percentage increase of improved land in farms[20]	...	...	...	...	...	...	...	159.9	47.6

General Population, Agriculture, and Manufacturing Statistics, 1790-1970

ILLINOIS

1880	1890	1900	1910	1920	1930	1940	1950	1960	1970
3,077,871	3,826,352	4,821,550	5,638,591	6,485,280	7,630,654	7,897,241	8,712,176	10,081,158	11,113,976
21.2	24.3	26.0	16.9	15.0	17.7	3.5	10.3	15.7	10.2
537,980	748,480	995,199	817,041	846,689	1,145,374	266,587	814,935	1,368,982	1,032,818
6.1	6.1	6.3	6.1	6.1	6.2	6.0	5.8	5.6	5.5
55.0	68.3	86.1	100.6	115.7	136.4	141.2	155.8	180.4	199.4
20	22	25	27	27	27	26	25	24	24
3,031,151	3,768,472	4,734,873	5,526,962	6,299,333	7,295,267	7,504,202	8,046,058	9,010,252	9,600,381
20.7	24.3	25.6	16.7	14.0	15.8	2.8	7.2	12.0	6.5
46,368	57,028	85,078	109,049	182,274	328,972	387,446	645,980	1,037,470	1,425,674
61.2	23.0	49.2	28.1	67.1	80.5	17.8	66.7	60.6	37.4
1.5	1.5	1.8	1.9	2.8	4.3	5.0	7.4	10.3	12.8
. . .	. . .	. . .	. . .	. . .	. . .	. . .	. . .	. . .	. . .
940,504	1,719,172	2,616,368	3,479,935	4,403,677	5,635,727	5,809,650	6,486,673[c] / 6,759,271[d]	7,650,582[c] / 8,140,315[d]	9,229,821[d]
57.8	82.8	52.2	33.0	26.5	28.0	3.1	11.7[c]	17.9[c] / 20.4[d]	13.4[d]
2,137,367	2,107,180	2,205,182	2,158,656	2,081,603	1,994,927	2,087,591	2,225,503[c] / 1,952,905[d]	2,430,576[c] / 1,940,843[d]	1,884,155[d]
10.0	-1.4	4.7	-2.1	-3.6	-4.2	4.6	6.6[c]	9.2[c] / -0.6[d]	-2.9[d]
30.6	44.9	54.3	61.7	67.9	73.9	73.6	74.5[c] / 77.6[d]	75.9[c] / 80.7[d]	83.0[d]
69.4	55.1	45.7	38.3	32.1	26.1	26.4	25.5[c] / 22.4[d]	24.1[c] / 19.3[d]	17.0[d]
255,741	240,681	264,151	251,872	237,181	214,497	213,439	195,268	154,644	123,565
31,673,645	30,498,277	32,794,728	32,522,937	31,974,775	30,695,339	31,032,572	30,978,495	30,327,261	29,913,190
26,115,154	25,669,060	27,699,219	28,048,323	27,294,533	. . .	. . .	. . .		
16,939,089	17,950,065	20,519,034	20,273,916	20,372,347	18,958,337	18,270,025	20,364,489	20,967,738	19,351,709
26.1	-5.9	9.8	-4.6	-5.8	-9.6	-4.9	-8.5	-20.8	2.3
22.4	-3.7	7.5	-0.8	-1.7	-4.0	1.1	-1.7	-2.1	-1.4
35.1	-1.7	7.9	1.3	-2.7					

General Population, Agriculture, and Manufacturing Statistics, 1790-1970—ILLINOIS (Cont.)

Item No.		1790 (or 1789)	1800	1810	1820	1830	1840	1850	1860	1870
26.	Average acreage per farm[18, 19]	...	...	...	...	...	...	158.0	145.9	127.6
27.	Percentage increase in cropland harvested[18, 19]	...	...	...	...	...	...	...	NA	NA
28.	Value of farms, dollars[18, 19]	...	...	...	...	...	...	96,133,290	408,944,033	736,405,077
29.	Value of farms, percent increase[18, 19]	...	...	...	...	...	...	...	325.4	80.1
30.	Average value per farm, dollars[18, 19]	...	...	...	...	...	...	1,261	2,854	3,631
31.	Farms operated by owners[21, 22, 23, 24, 25, 26, 27]	...	...	...	...	...	...	...	...	...
32.	Value of livestock on farms, dollars[28, 29, 30, 36]	...	...	...	...	...	...	.24,209,258	72,501,225	119,805,358[b]
33.	Average value of livestock per farm, dollars[19, 28, 29, 30, 36]	...	...	...	...	...	...	318	506	591[b]
34.	Production of wheat in bushels[31, 32, 35, 36]	...	...	...	...	...	3,335,393	9,414,575	23,837,028	30,128,405
35.	Percent of total production of wheat[31, 32, 33, 35, 36]	...	...	...	...	...	3.9	9.4	13.8	10.5
36.	Production of corn in bushels[36, 37, 38, 39]	...	...	...	...	...	...	57,646,984	115,174,777	129,921,395
37.	Percent of total production of corn[36, 37, 38, 39]	...	...	...	...	...	...	9.7	13.7	17.1
38.	Production of oats in bushels[31, 35, 36]	...	...	...	...	...	4,988,008	10,087,241	15,220,029	42,780,851
39.	Percent of total production of oats[31, 35, 36]	...	...	...	...	...	4.0	6.9	8.8	15.2
40.	Production of soybeans in bushels[36, 40, 41]	...	...	...	...	...	...	...	...	...
41.	Percent of total production of soybeans[36, 40, 41]	...	...	...	...	...	...	...	...	...
42.	Production of hay crops in tons[31, 34, 42, 43, 44]	...	...	...	...	...	164,932	601,952	1,774,554	2,747,339
43.	Percent of total production of hay crops[31, 34, 42, 43, 44]	...	...	...	...	...	1.6	4.4	9.3	10.1
44.	Number of manufacturing establishments[45, 46, 47, 48]	...	...	...	...	...	...	3,162	4,268	12,597
45.	Capital of manufacturing establishments[45, 46, 47, 48]	...	...	...	...	...	...	6,217,765	27,548,563	94,368,057
46.	Average number of wage earners[45, 46, 47, 48]	...	...	...	...	...	...	11,559	22,968	82,979
47.	Total wages[45, 46, 47, 48]	...	...	...	...	...	...	3,204,336	7,637,921	31,100,244
48.	Cost of materials used in manufacturing[45, 46, 47, 48]	...	...	...	...	...	...	8,959,327	35,558,782	127,600,077
49.	Value of manufactured product[45, 46, 47, 48]	...	...	...	...	...	...	16,534,272	57,580,886	205,620,672

a. Population of Illinois Territory
b. Values in gold
c. Previous definition of urban
d. Present definition of urban

General Population, Agriculture, and Manufacturing Statistics, 1790-1970—ILLINOIS (Cont.)

1880	1890	1900	1910	1920	1930	1940	1950	1960	1970
123.8	126.7	124.2	129.1	134.8	143.1	145.4	158.6	196.1	242.1
NA	6.0	14.3	-1.2	0.5	-6.9	-3.6	11.5	3.0	-7.7
1,009,594,580	1,262,870,587	1,765,581,550	3,522,792,570	5,997,993,566	3,336,049,028	2,537,117,306	5,394,905,000	9,579,602,000	14,643,393,000
37.1	25.1	39.8	99.5	70.3	-20.6	15.0	47.3	36.1	52.9
3,948	5,247	6,684	13,986	25,289	15,553	11,887	27,628	61,946	118,507
175,497	158,848	160,453	145,107	132,574	119,892	119,830	127,005	102,461	92,580
132,437,762	180,431,662	193,758,037	308,804,431	444,209,281	289,505,765	209,239,272	564,483,012	707,495,509	590,040,000
518	750	734	1,226	1,881	1,350	980	2,891	4,575	3,807
51,110,502	37,389,444	19,795,500	37,830,732	70,890,917	30,150,949	38,107,733	27,632,000	42,484,623	35,748,000
11.1	8.0	3.0	5.5	7.5	3.8	5.4	2.7	4.0	4.7
325,792,481	289,697,256	398,149,140	390,218,676	285,346,031	275,850,367	382,457,687	457,731,394	673,350,000	735,560,000
18.6	13.7	14.9	15.3	12.2	12.9	16.5	16.5	15.7	20.6
63,189,200	137,624,828	180,305,630	150,386,074	129,104,668	128,257,740	92,108,749	148,343,869	85,906,342	34,272,000
15.5	17.0	19.1	14.9	12.2	12.9	10.6	13.1	8.6	5.4
...	...	...	...	...	3,249,996	44,771,860	73,390,475	120,910,225	210,800,000
...	...	...	...	...	37.5	16.5	34.5	23.4	18.8
3,276,319	4,911,104	3,948,563	4,354,466	3,637,380	3,610,648	3,794,655	3,444,072	4,391,318	3,378,000
9.3	7.3	5.0	4.7	4.0	4.2	4.6	3.9	4.1	3.2
14,549	20,482	38,360	18,026	18,593	15,333	12,980			
140,652,066	502,004,512	776,829,598	1,548,171,000	3,366,453,000					
144,727	280,218	395,110	465,764	653,114	691,555	596,476			
57,429,085	142,873,265	191,510,962	273,319,000	801,087,000	1,024,870,000	750,239,000			
289,843,907	529,019,089	739,754,414	1,160,927,000	3,488,270,000	3,352,054,000	2,593,266,000			
414,864,673	908,640,280	1,259,730,168	1,919,277,000	5,425,245,000	6,282,092,000	4,794,861,000			

} See following tables

INDIANA

Item No.		1790 (or 1789)	1800	1810	1820	1830	1840	1850	1860	1870
1.	Population[1]	...	5,641[a]	24,520[a]	147,178	343,031	685,866	988,416	1,350,428	1,680,637
2.	Decennial rates of increase in population over preceding census[2]	...	...	334.7	500.2	133.1	99.9	44.1	36.6	24.5
3.	Increase in population over previous census[1, 3]	...	5,641	18,879	122,658	195,853	342,835	302,550	362,012	330,209
4.	Percent distribution of population[4]	....	0.1	0.3	1.5	2.7	4.0	4.3	4.3	4.4
5.	Population per square mile of land area[5, 6]	...b	...	...	...	...	...	27.5	37.6	46.8
6.	Membership of House of Representatives at each apportionment[7]	...	...	1	3	7	10	11	11	13
7.	White population[8, 9, 10]	...	5,343	23,890	145,758	339,399	678,698	977,154	1,338,710	1,655,837
8.	Percentage increase in white population over preceding census[9, 10, 11]	...	...	347.1	510.1	132.9	100.0	44.0	37.0	23.7
9.	Negro population[8, 9, 10]	...	298	630	1,420	3,632	7,168	11,262	11,428	24,560
10.	Percentage increase in Negro population over preceding census[9, 10, 11, 12, 13, 14]	...	...	111.4	125.4	155.8	97.4	57.1	1.5	114.9
11.	Percent Negro in total population[1, 8, 9, 10, 14, 15]	...	5.3	2.6	1.0	1.1	1.0	1.1	0.9	1.5
12.	Number of slaves in the area enumerated in 1790 and in the added area[16]	...	28	237	190	3	3	...	...	...
13.	Urban population[17]	...	...	...	...	...	10,716	44,632	115,904	247,657
14.	Percent urban increase over preceding census[17]	...	...	...	...	...	...	316.5	159.7	113.7
15.	Rural population[17]	...	5,641	24,520	147,178	343,031	675,150	943,784	1,234,524	1,432,980
16.	Percent rural increase over preceding census[17]	...	...	334.7	500.2	133.1	96.8	39.8	30.8	16.1
17.	Percent of urban to total population[17]	...	...	...	...	...	1.6	4.5	8.6	14.7
18.	Percent of rural to total population[17]	...	100	100	100	100	98.4	95.5	91.4	85.3
19.	Number of farms[18, 19]	...	...	...	...	...	...	93,896	131,826	161,289
20.	Acres in farms[18, 19]	...	...	...	...	...	...	12,793,422	16,388,292	18,119,648
21.	Acres improved land in farms[20]	...	...	...	...	...	...	5,046,543	8,242,183	10,104,279
22.	Cropland harvested, acres[18, 19]	...	...	...	...	...	...	...	...	...
23.	Percentage increase in number of farms[18, 19]	...	...	...	...	...	...	...	40.4	22.3
24.	Percentage increase of land in farms[18, 19]	...	...	...	...	...	...	...	28.1	10.6
25.	Percentage increase of improved land in farms[20]	...	...	...	...	...	...	...	63.3	22.6

General Population, Agriculture, and Manufacturing Statistics, 1790-1970

INDIANA

1880	1890	1900	1910	1920	1930	1940	1950	1960	1970
1,978,301	2,192,404	2,516,462	2,700,876	2,930,390	3,238,503	3,427,796	3,934,224	4,662,498	5,193,669
17.7	10.8	14.8	7.3	8.5	10.5	5.8	14.8	18.5	11.4
297,664	214,103	324,058	184,414	229,514	308,113	189,293	506,428	728,274	531,171
3.9	3.5	3.3	2.9	2.8	2.6	2.6	2.6	2.6	2.6
55.1	61.1	70.1	74.9	81.3	89.4	94.7	108.7	128.8	143.9
13	13	13	13	13	12	11	11	11	11
1,938,798	2,146,736	2,458,502	2,639,961	2,849,071	3,125,778	3,305,323	3,758,512	4,388,554	4,820,324
17.1	10.7	14.5	7.4	7.9	9.7	5.7	13.7	16.8	9.8
39,228	45,215	57,505	60,320	80,810	111,982	121,916	174,168	269,275	357,464
59.7	15.3	27.2	4.9	34.0	38.6	8.9	42.8	54.6	32.7
2.0	2.1	2.3	2.2	2.8	3.5	3.6	4.4	5.8	6.9
. . .	. . .	. . .	. . .	. . .	. . .	. . .	. . .	. . .	. . .
386,211	590,039	862,689	1,143,835	1,482,855	1,795,892	1,887,712	2,217,468[c] / 2,357,196[d]	2,650,378[c] / 2,910,149[d]	3,372,060[d]
55.9	52.8	46.2	32.6	29.6	21.1	5.1	17.5[c] / 23.5[d]	19.5[c] / 23.5[d]	15.9[d]
1,592,090	1,602,365	1,653,773	1,557,041	1,447,535	1,442,611	1,540,084	1,716,756[c] / 1,577,028[d]	2,012,120[c] / 1,752,349[d]	1,821,609[d]
11.1	0.6	3.2	-5.8	-7.0	-0.3	6.8	11.5[c]	17.2[c] / 11.1[d]	4.0[d]
19.5	26.9	34.3	42.4	50.6	55.5	55.1	56.4[c] / 59.9[d]	56.8[c] / 62.4[d]	64.9[d]
80.5	73.1	65.7	57.6	49.4	44.5	44.9	43.6[c] / 40.1[d]	43.2[c] / 37.6[d]	35.1[d]
194,013	198,167	221,897	215,485	205,126	181,570	184,549	166,627	128,160	101,479
20,420,983	20,362,516	21,619,623	21,299,823	21,063,332	19,688,675	19,800,778	19,658,677	18,613,046	17,573,000
13,933,738	15,107,482	16,680,358	16,931,252	16,680,212	. . .	. . .	. . .	. . .	. . .
8,261,961	9,812,393	11,134,726	11,331,395	11,850,661	10,213,813	9,711,028	11,000,662	11,147,102	9,670,494
20.3	2.1	12.0	-2.9	2.8	3.5	3.6	4.5		
12.7	-0.3	6.2	-1.5	-1.1	-1.1	-3.5	-1.8	-3.2	-5.6
37.9	8.4	10.4	1.5	-1.5	. . .	. . .	. . .	. . .	. . .

General Population, Agriculture, and Manufacturing Statistics, 1790-1970—INDIANA (Cont.)

Item No.		1790 (or 1789)	1800	1810	1820	1830	1840	1850	1860	1870
26.	Average acreage per farm[18, 19]	. . .	. . .	. . .	. . .	. . .	. . .	1362	124.3	112.3
27.	Percentage increase in cropland harvested[18, 19]	. . .	. . .	. . .	. . .	. . .	. . .	. . .	NA	NA
28.	Value of farms, dollars[18, 19]	. . .	. . .	. . .	. . .	. . .	. . .	136,385,173	356,712,175	507,843,351
29.	Value of farms, percent increase[18, 19]	. . .	. . .	. . .	. . .	. . .	. . .	. . .	161.5	42.4
30.	Average value per farm, dollars[18, 19]	. . .	. . .	. . .	. . .	. . .	. . .	1,453	2,706	3,149
31.	Farms operated by owners[21, 22, 23, 24, 25, 26, 27]	. . .	. . .	. . .	. . .	. . .	. . .	. . .	. . .	. . .
32.	Value of livestock on farms, dollars[28, 29, 30, 36]	. . .	. . .	. . .	. . .	. . .	. . .	22,478,555	41,855,539	67,021,426[b]
33.	Average value of livestock per farm, dollars[19, 28, 29, 30, 36]	. . .	. . .	. . .	. . .	. . .	. . .	239	318	416[b]
34.	Production of wheat in bushels[31, 32, 35, 36]	. . .	. . .	. . .	. . .	. . .	4,049,375	6,214,458	16,848,267	27,747,222
35.	Percent of total production of wheat[31, 32, 33, 35, 36]	. . .	. . .	. . .	. . .	. . .	4.0	6.2	9.7	9.6
36.	Production of corn in bushels[36, 37, 38, 39]	. . .	. . .	. . .	. . .	. . .	. . .	52,964,363	71,588,919	51,094,538
37.	Percent of total production of corn[36, 37, 38, 39]	. . .	. . .	. . .	. . .	. . .	. . .	8.9	8.5	6.7
38.	Production of oats in bushels[31, 35, 36]	. . .	. . .	. . .	. . .	. . .	5,981,605	5,655,014	5,317,831	8,590,409
39.	Percent of total production of oats[31, 35, 36]	. . .	. . .	. . .	. . .	. . .	4.9	3.9	3.1	3.1
40.	Production of soybeans in bushels[36, 40, 41]	. . .	. . .	. . .	. . .	. . .	. . .	. . .	. . .	. . .
41.	Percent of total production of soybeans[36, 40, 41]	. . .	. . .	. . .	. . .	. . .	. . .	. . .	. . .	. . .
42.	Production of hay crops in tons[31, 34, 42, 43, 44]	. . .	. . .	. . .	. . .	. . .	178,029	403,230	622,426	1,076,768
43.	Percent of total production of hay crops[31, 34, 42, 43, 44]	. . .	. . .	. . .	. . .	. . .	. . .	2.9	3.3	3.9
44.	Number of manufacturing establishments[45, 46, 47, 48]	. . .	. . .	. . .	. . .	. . .	. . .	4,392	5,323	11,847
45.	Capital of manufacturing establishments[45, 46, 47, 48]	. . .	. . .	. . .	. . .	. . .	. . .	7,750,402	18,451,121	52,052,425
46.	Average number of wage earners[45, 46, 47, 48]	. . .	. . .	. . .	. . .	. . .	. . .	14,440	21,295	58,852
47.	Total wages[45, 46, 47, 48]	. . .	. . .	. . .	. . .	. . .	. . .	3,728,844	6,318,335	18,366,780
48.	Cost of materials used in manufacturing[45, 46, 47, 48]	. . .	. . .	. . .	. . .	. . .	. . .	10,369,700	27,142,597	63,135,492
49.	Value of manufactured product[45, 46, 47, 48]	. . .	. . .	. . .	. . .	. . .	. . .	18,725,423	42,803,469	108,617,278

a. 1800 figure includes population of those portions of Indiana Territory which were taken to form Michigan and Illinois Territories in 1805 and 1809, respectively, and that portion which was separated in1816. 1810 figure includes population of area separated in 1816.

b. Values in gold

c. Previous urban definition

d. Present urban definition

1880	1890	1900	1910	1920	1930	1940	1950	1960	1970
105.3	102.8	97.4	98.8	102.7	108.4	107.3	118.0	145.2	173.2
NA	18.8	13.5	1.8	4.6	-13.8	-4.9	13.3	1.3	-13.2
635,236,111	754,789,110	841,735,340	1,594,275,596	2,653,643,973	1,415,542,192	1,251,491,614	2,691,273,000	4,932,749,000	7,135,620,000
25.1	18.8	11.5	89.4	66.4	-16.5	20.3	50.0	32.1	44.6
3,274	3,809	3,793	7,899	12,937	7,796	6,781	16,151	38,489	70,316
147,963	147,885	158,449	148,501	137,210	125,517	131,263	133,980	106,047	89,105
71,068,758	93,361,422	109,550,761	173,860,101	260,372,580	175,235,615	134,156,789	331,212,725	408,035,166	354,830,000
366	471	494	807	1,274	965	726	1,988	3,184	3,513
47,284,853	37,318,798	34,986,280	33,935,972	45,207,862	25,190,384	25,653,913	32,193,000	30,941,720	29,799,000
10.3	8.0	5.3	5.0	4.8	3.1	3.6	3.2	2.9	2.2
115,482,300	108,843,094	178,967,070	195,496,433	158,603,938	114,871,320	187,635,164	219,032,305	325,314,000	371,998,000
6.6	5.1	6.7	7.6	6.8	5.4	8.1	7.9	7.6	9.1
15,599,518	31,491,661	34,565,070	50,607,913	52,529,723	47,465,387	22,607,221	48,759,882	33,428,856	15,423,000
3.8	3.9	3.7	5.0	5.0	4.8	2.6	4.3	3.3	1.7
...	...	...	...	...	1,379,279	13,763,282	30,818,984	58,440,247	101,618,000
...	...	...	...	...	15.9	15.7	14.5	11.3	9.0
1,361,083	2,741,045	2,905,608	2,880,104	2,280,863	2,450,101	2,637,420	2,160,180	2,510,632	2,204,000
3.9	4.1	3.7	2.9	2.5	2.0	3.2	2.4	2.4	1.7
11,198	12,354	18,015	7,969	7,916	5,091	4,337	See following tables		
65,742,962	131,605,366	234,481,528	508,717,000	1,335,714,000	...	...			
69,508	110,590	155,956	186,984	277,580	314,698	277,467			
21,960,888	42,577,258	66,847,317	95,510,000	317,043,000	418,771,000	345,475,000			
100,262,917	130,119,106	214,961,610	333,375,000	1,174,951,000	1,403,431,000	1,257,436,000			
148,006,411	226,825,082	378,120,140	579,075,000	1,898,753,000	2,539,894,000	2,227,648,000			

General Population, Agriculture, and Manufacturing Statistics, 1790-1970

IOWA

Item No.		1790 (or 1789)	1800	1810	1820	1830	1840	1850	1860	1870
1.	Population[1]	. . .	. . .	. . .	. . .	. . .	43,112[a]	192,214	674,913	1,194,020
2.	Decennial rates of increase in population over preceding census[2]	. . .	. . .	. . .	. . .	. . .	. . .	345.8	251.1	76.9
3.	Increase in population over previous census[1, 3]	. . .	. . .	. . .	. . .	. . .	43,112	149,102	482,699	519,107
4.	Percent distribution of population[4]	. . .	. . .	. . .	. . .	. . .	0.3	0.8	2.1	3.1
5.	Population per square mile of land area[5, 6]	. . .	. . .	. . .	. . .	. . .	. . .	3.5	12.1	21.5
6.	Membership of House of Representatives at each apportionment[7]	. . .	. . .	. . .	. . .	. . .	2	2	6	9
7.	White population[8, 9, 10]	. . .	. . .	. . .	. . .	. . .	42,924	191,881	673,779	1,188,207
8.	Percentage increase in white population over preceding census[9, 10, 11]	. . .	. . .	. . .	. . .	. . .	. . .	347.0	251.1	76.3
9.	Negro population[8, 9, 10]	. . .	. . .	. . .	. . .	. . .	188	333	1,069	5,762
10.	Percentage increase in Negro population over preceding census[9, 10, 11, 12, 13, 14]	. . .	. . .	. . .	. . .	. . .	. . .	77.1	221.0	439.0
11.	Percent Negro in total population[1, 8, 9, 10, 14, 15]	. . .	. . .	. . .	. . .	. . .	0.3	0.2	0.2	0.5
12.	Number of slaves in the area enumerated in 1790 and in the added area[16]	. . .	. . .	. . .	. . .	. . .	16	. . .	. . .	
13.	Urban population[17]	. . .	. . .	. . .	. . .	. . .	. . .	9,730	60,028	156,327
14.	Percent urban increase over preceding census[17]	. . .	. . .	. . .	. . .	. . .	. . .	. . .	516.9	160.4
15.	Rural population[17]	. . .	. . .	. . .	. . .	. . .	43,112	182,484	614,885	1,037,693
16.	Percent rural increase over preceding census[17]	. . .	. . .	. . .	. . .	. . .	. . .	323.3	237.0	68.8
17.	Percent of urban to total population[17]	. . .	. . .	. . .	. . .	. . .	. . .	5.1	8.9	13.1
18.	Percent of rural to total population[17]	. . .	. . .	. . .	. . .	. . .	100.0	94.9	91.1	86.9
19.	Number of farms[18, 19]	. . .	. . .	. . .	. . .	. . .	. . .	14,805	61,163	116,292
20.	Acres in farms[18, 19]	. . .	. . .	. . .	. . .	. . .	. . .	2,736,064	10,069,907	15,541,793
21.	Acres improved land in farms[20]	. . .	. . .	. . .	. . .	. . .	. . .	824,682	3,792,792	9,396,467
22.	Cropland harvested, acres[18, 19]	. . .	. . .	. . .	. . .	. . .	. . .	NA	NA	NA
23.	Percentage increase in number of farms[18, 19]	. . .	. . .	. . .	. . .	. . .	. . .	. . .	313.1	90.1
24.	Percentage increase of land in farms[18, 19]	. . .	. . .	. . .	. . .	. . .	. . .	. . .	268.0	54.3
25.	Percentage increase of improved land in farms[20]	. . .	. . .	. . .	. . .	. . .	. . .	. . .	359.9	147.7

General Population, Agriculture, and Manufacturing Statistics, 1790-1970

IOWA

1880	1890	1900	1910	1920	1930	1940	1950	1960	1970
1,624,615	1,912,297	2,231,853	2,224,771	2,404,021	2,470,939	2,538,268	2,621,073	2,757,537	2,824,376
36.1	17.7	16.7	-0.3	8.1	2.8	2.7	3.3	5.2	2.4
430,595	287,281	319,556	-7,082	17,925	66,918	67,329	82,805	136,464	66,839
3.2	3.0	2.9	2.4	2.3	2.0	1.9	1.7	1.5	1.4
29.2	34.4	40.2	40.0	43.2	44.5	45.3	46.8	49.2	50.5
11	11	11	11	11	9	8	8	7	6
1,614,600	1,901,090	2,218,667	2,209,191	2,384,181	2,452,677	2,520,691	2,599,546	2,728,709	2,782,762
35.9	17.7	16.7	-0.4	7.9	2.8	2.8	3.1	5.0	2.0
9,516	10,685	12,693	14,973	19,005	17,380	16,694	19,692	25,354	32,596
65.2	12.3	18.8	18.0	26.9	-8.6	-3.9	17.9	28.7	28.6
0.6	0.6	0.6	0.7	0.8	0.7	0.7	0.8	0.9	1.2
. . .	. . .	. . .	. . .	. . .	. . .	. . .	. . .	. . .	. . .
247,427	405,764	572,386	680,054	875,495	979,292	1,084,231	1,229,433[c] 1,250,938[d]	1,439,525[c] 1,462,512[d]	1,616,405[d]
58.3	64.0	41.1	18.8	28.7	11.9	10.7	13.4[c]	17.1[c] 16.9[d]	10.5[d]
1,377,188	1,506,533	1,659,467	1,544,717	1,528,526	1,491,647	1,454,037	1,391,640[c] 1,370,135[d]	1,318,012[c] 1,295,025[d]	1,207,971[d]
32.7	9.4	10.2	-6.9	-1.0	-2.4	-2.5	-4.3	-5.3[c] -5.5[d]	-6.7[d]
15.2	21.2	25.6	30.6	36.4	39.6	42.7	46.9[c] 47.7[d]	52.2[c] 53.0[d]	57.2[d]
84.8	78.8	74.4	69.4	63.6	60.4	57.3	53.1[c] 52.3[d]	47.8[c] 47.0[d]	42.8[d]
185,351	201,903	228,622	217,044	213,439	214,928	213,318	203,159	174,707	140,354
24,752,700	30,491,541	34,574,337	33,930,688	33,474,896	34,019,332	34,148,673	34,264,639	33,830,950	33,569,629
19,866,541	25,428,899	29,897,552	29,491,199	28,606,951					
13,982,995	18,219,553	21,985,377	20,374,925	20,422,591	22,275,868	20,076,641	22,547,337	22,873,407	19,286,658
59.4	8.9	13.2	-5.1	-1.7	0.7	-0.7	-4.8	-14.0	-20.0
59.3	23.2	13.4	-1.9	-1.3	2.2	-0.6	-0.5	-0.6	
111.4	28.0	17.6	-1.4	-3.0					

General Population, Agriculture, and Manufacturing Statistics, 1790-1970—IOWA (Cont.)

Item No.	1790 (or 1789)	1800	1810	1820	1830	1840	1850	1860	1870
26. Average acreage per farm[18, 19]	. . .	. . .	. . .	. . .	. . .	. . .	184.8	164.6	133.6
27. Percentage increase in cropland harvested[18, 19]	. . .	. . .	. . .	. . .	. . .	. . .	. . .	. . .	. . .
28. Value of farms, dollars[18, 19]	. . .	. . .	. . .	. . .	. . .	. . .	16,657,567	119,899,547	314,129,953
29. Value of farms, percent increase[18, 19]	. . .	. . .	. . .	. . .	. . .	. . .	. . .	619.8	162.0
30. Average value per farm, dollars[18, 19]	. . .	. . .	. . .	. . .	. . .	. . .	1,125	1,960	2,701
31. Farms operated by owners[21, 22, 23, 24, 25, 26, 27]	. . .	. . .	. . .	. . .	. . .	. . .	. . .	. . .	. . .
32. Value of livestock on farms, dollars[28, 29, 30, 36]	. . .	. . .	. . .	. . .	. . .	. . .	3,689,275	22,476,293	66,389,706
33. Average value of livestock per farm, dollars[19, 28, 29, 30, 36]	. . .	. . .	. . .	. . .	. . .	. . .	249	367	571
34. Production of wheat in bushels[31, 32, 35, 36]	. . .	. . .	. . .	. . .	. . .	154,693	1,530,581	8,449,403	29,435,692
35. Percent of total production of wheat[31, 32, 33, 35, 36]	. . .	. . .	. . .	. . .	. . .	. . .	1.5	4.9	10.2
36. Production of corn in bushels[36, 37, 38, 39]	. . .	. . .	. . .	. . .	. . .	. . .	8,656,799	42,410,686	68,935,065
37. Percent of total production of corn[36, 37, 38, 39]	. . .	. . .	. . .	. . .	. . .	. . .	1.5	5.0	9.1
38. Production of oats in bushels[31, 35, 36]	. . .	. . .	. . .	. . .	. . .	216,385	1,524,345	5,887,645	21,005,142
39. Percent of total production of oats[31, 35, 36]	. . .	. . .	. . .	. . .	. . .	0.1	1.0	3.4	7.4
40. Production of soybeans in bushels[36, 40, 41]	. . .	. . .	. . .	. . .	. . .	. . .	. . .	. . .	. . .
41. Percent of total production of soybeans[36, 40, 41]	. . .	. . .	. . .	. . .	. . .	. . .	. . .	. . .	. . .
42. Production of hay crops in tons[31, 42, 43, 44]	. . .	. . .	. . .	. . .	. . .	17,953	89,055	813,173	1,777,339
43. Percent of total production of hay crops[31, 34, 42, 43, 44]	. . .	. . .	. . .	. . .	. . .	. . .	0.6	4.3	6.5
44. Number of manufacturing establishments[45, 46, 47, 48]	. . .	. . .	. . .	. . .	. . .	. . .	522	1,939	6,566
45. Capital of manufacturing establishments[45, 46, 47, 48]	. . .	. . .	. . .	. . .	. . .	. . .	1,292,875	7,247,130	22,420,183
46. Average number of wage earners[45, 46, 47, 48]	. . .	. . .	. . .	. . .	. . .	. . .	1,707	6,307	25,032
47. Total wages[45, 46, 47, 48]	. . .	. . .	. . .	. . .	. . .	. . .	473,016	1,922,417	6,893,292
48. Cost of materials used in manufacturing[45, 46, 47, 48]	. . .	. . .	. . .	. . .	. . .	. . .	2,356,881	8,612,259	27,682,096
49. Value of manufactured product[45, 46, 47, 48]	. . .	. . .	. . .	. . .	. . .	. . .	3,551,783	13,971,325	46,534,322

a. Includes population of area constituting that part of Minnesota lying west of the Mississippi River and a line drawn from its source northwards to the Canadian boundary.

b. Values in gold

c. Previous definition of urban

d. Present definition of urban

General Population, Agriculture, and Manufacturing Statistics, 1790-1970—IOWA (Cont.)

1880	1890	1900	1910	1920	1930	1940	1950	1960	1970
133.5	151.0	151.2	156.3	156.8	158.3	160.1	168.7	193.6	239.2
. . .	30.3	20.7	-7.3	0.2	3.8	6.1	4.6	1.9	-15.7
567,430,227	857,581,022	1,497,554,790	3,257,379,400	7,601,772,290	4,224,506,083	2,690,744,215	5,506,670,000	8,856,924,000	13,150,363,000
80.6	51.1	74.6	117.5	133.4	-14.7	9.3	52.5	26.8	53.1
3,061	4,247	6,550	15,008	35,616	19,655	12,614	27,105	49,150	93,694
141,177	145,183	148,886	133,003	121,888	111,333	110,616	125,062	113,223	106,605
124,715,103	206,436,242	278,830,096	393,003,196	611,821,643	496,965,755	335,772,837	889,797,868	1,236,974,635	1,383,430,000
673	1,022	1,220	1,811	2,876	2,312	1,574	4,380	7,080	19,721
31,154,205	8,249,786	22,769,440	8,055,944	21,591,928	7,990,286	6,567,597	5,454,000	3,257,682	1,400,000
6.8	1.8	3.5	1.2	2.3	1.0	1.0	0.5	0.3	0.1
275,014,247	313,130,782	383,453,190	341,750,460	371,362,393	389,000,414	469,786,611	503,589,858	811,265,000	859,140,000
15.7	14.8	14.4	13.4	15.8	18.3	20.3	18.1	18.9	21.0
50,610,591	146,679,289	168,364,170	128,198,055	187,045,705	208,070,091	155,348,088	233,533,684	184,086,771	94,105,000
12.4	18.1	17.8	12.7	17.7	21.0	17.9	20.5	18.4	10.3
. . .	. . .	. . .	. . .	. . .	573,711	11,359,475	29,596,245	62,106,812	184,600,000
. . .	. . .	. . .	. . .	. . .	6.6	13.0	13.9	12.0	16.4
3,613,941	7,264,700	6,174,686	7,312,591	5,348,102	5,384,422	5,051,371	4,830,842	8,140,050	6,910,000
10.3	10.9	8.7	8.4	5.9	6.3	6.1	5.4	7.6	5.4
6,921	7,440	14,819	5,528	5,683	3,317	2,670			
33,987,886	77,513,097	102,733,103	171,219,000	403,206,000					
28,372	51,037	58,553	61,635	80,551	81,678	65,314			
9,725,962	20,429,620	23,931,680	32,542,000	90,117,000	102,327,000	73,466,000			
48,704,311	79,292,407	101,170,357	170,707,000	520,241,000	574,394,000	473,737,000			
71,045,926	125,049,183	164,617,877	259,238,000	745,473,000	898,213,000	718,532,000			

KANSAS

Item No.	1790 (or 1789)	1800	1810	1820	1830	1840	1850	1860	1870
1. Population[1]	. . .	. . .	. . .	. . .	. . .	. . .	. . .	107,206	364,39▸
2. Decennial rates of increase in population over preceding census[2]	. . .	. . .	. . .	. . .	. . .	. . .	. . .	. . .	239.9
3. Increase in population over previous census[1, 3]	. . .	. . .	. . .	. . .	. . .	. . .	. . .	107,206	257,193
4. Percent distribution of population[4]	. . .	. . .	. . .	. . .	. . .	. . .	. . .	0.3	0.9
5. Population per square mile of land area[5, 6]	. . .	. . .	. . .	. . .	. . .	. . .	. . .	1.3	4.5
6. Membership of House of Representatives at each apportionment[7]	. . .	. . .	. . .	. . .	. . .	. . .	. . .	1	3
7. White population[8, 9, 10]	. . .	. . .	. . .	. . .	. . .	. . .	. . .	106,390	346,377
8. Percentage increase in white population over preceding census[9, 10, 11]	. . .	. . .	. . .	. . .	. . .	. . .	. . .	. . .	225.6
9. Negro population[8, 9, 10]	. . .	. . .	. . .	. . .	. . .	. . .	. . .	627	17,108
10. Percentage increase in Negro population over preceding census[9, 10, 11, 12, 13, 14]	. . .	. . .	. . .	. . .	. . .	. . .	. . .	. . .	2,628.5
11. Percent Negro in total population[1, 8, 9, 10, 14, 15]	. . .	. . .	. . .	. . .	. . .	. . .	. . .	0.6	4.7
12. Number of slaves in the area enumerated in 1790 and in the added area[16]	. . .	. . .	. . .	. . .	. . .	. . .	. . .	2	. . .
13. Urban population[17]	. . .	. . .	. . .	. . .	. . .	. . .	. . .	10,045	51,870
14. Percent urban increase over preceding census[17]	. . .	. . .	. . .	. . .	. . .	. . .	. . .	. . .	416.4
15. Rural population[17]	. . .	. . .	. . .	. . .	. . .	. . .	. . .	97,161	312,529
16. Percent rural increase over preceding census[17]	. . .	. . .	. . .	. . .	. . .	. . .	. . .	221.7	221.7
17. Percent of urban to total population[17]	. . .	. . .	. . .	. . .	. . .	. . .	. . .	9.4	14.2
18. Percent of rural to total population[17]	. . .	. . .	. . .	. . .	. . .	. . .	. . .	90.6	85.8
19. Number of farms[18, 19]	. . .	. . .	. . .	. . .	. . .	. . .	. . .	10,400	38,202
20. Acres in farms[18, 19]	. . .	. . .	. . .	. . .	. . .	. . .	. . .	1,778,400	5,656,879
21. Acres improved land in farms[20]	. . .	. . .	. . .	. . .	. . .	. . .	. . .	405,468	1,971,003
22. Cropland harvested, acres[18, 19]	. . .	. . .	. . .	. . .	. . .	. . .	. . .	NA	NA
23. Percentage increase in number of farms[18, 19]	. . .	. . .	. . .	. . .	. . .	. . .	. . .	. . .	267.3
24. Percentage increase of land in farms[18, 19]	. . .	. . .	. . .	. . .	. . .	. . .	. . .	. . .	218.1
25. Percentage increase of improved land in farms[20]	. . .	. . .	. . .	. . .	. . .	. . .	. . .	. . .	386.1

General Population, Agriculture, and Manufacturing Statistics, 1790-1970

KANSAS

	1880	1890	1900	1910	1920	1930	1940	1950	1960	1970
	996,096	1,428,108	1,470,495	1,690,949	1,769,257	1,880,999	1,801,028	1,905,299	2,178,611	2,246,578
	173.4	43.4	3.0	15.0	4.6	6.3	-4.3	5.8	14.3	3.1
	631,697	431,000	42,387	220,454	78,308	111,742	-79,971	104,271	273,312	67,967
	2.0	2.3	1.9	1.8	1.7	1.5	1.4	1.3	1.2	1.1
	12.2	17.5	18.0	20.7	21.6	22.9	21.9	23.2	26.6	27.5
	7	8	8	8	8	7	6	6	5	5
	952,155	1,376,619	1,416,319	1,634,352	1,708,906	1,811,997	1,734,496	1,828,961	2,078,666	2,122,068
	174.9	44.6	2.9	15.4	4.6	6.0	-4.2	5.4	13.7	2.1
	43,107	49,710	52,003	54,030	57,925	66,344	65,138	73,158	91,445	106,977
	152.0	15.3	4.6	3.9	7.2	14.5	-1.8	1.2	25.00	17.0
	4.3	3.5	3.5	3.2	3.3	3.5	3.6	3.8	4.2	4.8
	. . .	. . .	. . .	. . .	. . .	. . .	. . .	. . .	. . .	. . .
	104,956	269,539	329,696	492,312	616,485	729,834	753,941	903,468[c] 993,220[d]	1,228,646[c] 1,328,741[d]	1,484,870[d]
	102.3	156.8	22.3	49.3	25.2	18.4	3.3	19.8[c]	36.0[c] 33.8[d]	11.8[d]
	891,140	1,158,569	1,140,799	1,198,637	1,152,772	1,151,165	1,047,087	1,001,831[c] 912,079[d]	949,965[c] 849,870[d]	761,708[d]
	185.1	30.0	-1.5	5.1	-3.8	-0.1	-9.0	-4.3[c]	-5.2[c] -6.8[d]	-10.4[d]
	10.5	18.9	22.4	29.1	34.8	38.8	41.9	47.4[c] 52.1[d]	56.4[c] 61.0[d]	66.1[d]
	89.5	81.1	77.6	70.9	65.2	61.2	58.1	52.6[c] 47.9[d]	43.6[c] 39.0[d]	33.9[d]
	138,561	166,617	173,098	177,841	165,286	166,042	156,327	131,394	104,347	86,057
	21,417,468	30,214,456	41,662,970	43,384,799	45,425,179	46,975,647	48,173,635	48,611,366	50,152,870	49,390,369
	10,739,566	22,303,301	25,040,550	29,904,067	30,600,760	. . .	. . .	21,493,734	20,528,357	17,649,231
	7,063,676	14,618,304	18,077,048	19,900,750	21,908,887	24,308,361	17,816,498	21,493,734	20,528,357	17,649,231
	262.7	20.2	3.9	2.7	-7.1	0.1	-10.5	-6.9	-13.2	-17.6
	278.6	41.1	37.9	4.1	4.7	7.4	0.3	-1.0	0.3	-0.1
	444.9	107.7	12.3	19.4	2.3	. . .	. . .	. . .	. . .	. . .

General Population, Agriculture, and Manufacturing Statistics, 1790-1970—KANSAS (Cont.)

Item No.	1790 (or 1789)	1800	1810	1820	1830	1840	1850	1860	1870
26. Average acreage per farm[18,19]	...	...	...	...	...	...	...	171.0	148.0
27. Percentage increase in cropland harvested[18,19]	...	...	...	...	...	...	...	NA	NA
28. Value of farms, dollars[18,19]	...	...	...	...	...	...	...	12,258,239	72,261,632
29. Value of farms, percent increase[18,19]	...	...	...	...	...	...	...	...	489.5
30. Average value per farm, dollars[18,19]	...	...	...	...	...	...	...	1,179	1,892
31. Farms operated by owners[21,22,23,24,25,26,27]	...	...	...	...	...	...	...	...	...
32. Value of livestock on farms, dollars[28,29,30,36]	...	...	...	...	...	...	...	3,332,450	18,538,548[b]
33. Average value of livestock per farm, dollars[19,28,29,30,36]	...	...	...	...	...	...	...	320	480[b]
34. Production of wheat in bushels[31,32,35,36]	...	...	...	...	...	...	...	194,173	2,391,198
35. Percent of total production of wheat[31,32,33,35,36]	...	...	...	...	...	...	...	0.1	0.8
36. Production of corn in bushels[36,37,38,39]	...	...	...	...	...	...	...	6,150,727	17,025,525
37. Percent of total production of corn[36,37,38,39]	...	...	...	...	...	...	...	0.7	2.2
38. Production of oats in bushels[31,35,36]	...	...	...	...	...	...	...	88,325	4,097,925
39. Percent of total production of oats[31,35,36]	...	...	...	...	...	...	...	...	1.5
40. Production of soybeans in bushels[36,40,41]	...	...	...	...	...	...	...	...	...
41. Percent of total production of soybeans[36,40,41]	...	...	...	...	...	...	...	...	...
42. Production of hay crops in tons[31,34,42,43,44]	...	...	...	...	...	...	...	56,232	490,289
43. Percent of total production of hay crops[31,34,42,43,44]	...	...	...	...	...	...	...	0.3	1.8
44. Number of manufacturing establishments[45,46,47,48]	...	...	...	...	...	...	...	344	1,477
45. Capital of manufacturing establishments[45,46,47,48]	...	...	...	...	...	...	...	1,084,935	4,319,060
46. Average number of wage earners[45,46,47,48]	...	...	...	...	...	...	...	1,735	6,844
47. Total wages[45,46,47,48]	...	...	...	...	...	...	...	880,346	2,377,511
48. Cost of materials used in manufacturing[45,46,47,48]	...	...	...	...	...	...	...	1,444,975	6,112,163
49. Value of manufactured product[45,46,47,48]	...	...	...	...	...	...	...	4,357,408	11,775,833

b. Values in gold

c. Previous definition of urban

d. Present definition of urban

1880	1890	1900	1910	1920	1930	1940	1950	1960	1970
154.6	181.3	240.7	244.0	274.8	282.9	308.2	370.0	480.6	574.0
NA	107.0	23.7	10.1	10.1	8.6	6.9	-5.8	-4.3	-14.0
235,178,936	559,726,046	643,652,770	1,737,556,172	2,830,063,918	2,281,101,631	1,421,387,464	3,198,628,000	5,017,473,000	7,842,501,000
225.4	138.0	15.0	170.0	62.9	3.8	-3.9	62.3	26.1	56.3
1,697	3,359	3,718	9,770	17,122	13,738	9,092	24,344	48,084	91,131
115,910	119,576	112,172	111,108	97,090	94,762	85,475	91,815	77,949	70,152
62,704,149	128,068,305	190,956,936	253,523,577	316,548,160	246,394,684	138,722,051	459,386,405	589,746,446	1,022,720,000
453	769	1,103	1,426	1,924	1,484	887	3,496	5,652	11,892
17,324,141	30,399,871	38,778,450	77,577,115	148,475,729	148,482,595	112,413,657	178,060,000	199,604,763	299,013,000
3.8	6.5	5.9	11.4	15.7	18.5	15.8	17.5	18.9	21.8
105,729,325	259,574,568	229,937,430	154,651,703	59,719,831	101,355,511	31,880,109	61,785,287	81,630,000	79,670,000
6.0	12.2	8.6	6.0	2.5	4.7	13.8	22.2	19.1	19.4
8,180,385	44,629,034	24,469,980	22,923,641	36,257,356	21,526,565	20,929,707	15,145,436	16,080,168	10,250,000
2.0	5.5	2.6	2.3	3.4	2.2	2.4	1.1	1.5	1.1
...	...	...	...	...	29,906	88,322	3,577,605	8,715,280	15,075,000
...	...	...	...	...	...	0.1	1.7	1.7	1.3
1,601,932	4,854,960	7,066,671	5,936,997	7,378,683	2,628,183	1,389,193	3,167,662	3,388,855	4,102,000
4.6	7.3	6.1	5.4	4.8	3.1	1.7	3.6	3.2	3.2
2,803	4,471	7,830	3,435	3,474	1,916	1,494			
11,192,315	43,926,002	66,827,362	156,090,000	357,534,000	...	...			
12,062	28,237	35,193	44,215	61,049	47,373	31,614			
3,995,010	13,288,175	16,317,689	25,904,000	73,060,000	63,348,000	36,938,000		See following tables	
21,453,141	78,845,167	129,485,320	258,884,000	750,088,000	546,247,000	345,401,000			
30,843,777	110,219,805	172,129,398	325,104,000	913,667,000	751,613,000	464,354,000			

17

General Population, Agriculture, and Manufacturing Statistics, 1790-1970

MICHIGAN

Item No.		1790 (or 1789)	1800	1810	1820	1830	1840	1850	1860	1870
1.	Population[1]	. . .	. . .	4,762	8,896	31,639	212,267	397,654	749,113	1,184,059
2.	Decennial rates of increase in population over preceding census[2]	. . .	. . .	. . .	86.8	255.7	570.9	87.3	88.4	58.1
3.	Increase in population over previous census[1, 3]	. . .	. . .	4,762	4,134	22,743	180,628	185,387	351,459	434,946
4.	Percent distribution of population[4]	. . .	. . .	0.1	0.1	0.2	1.2	1.7	2.4	3.1
5.	Population per square mile of land area[5, 6]	. . .	. . .	. . .	. . .	. . .	. . .	6.9	13.0	20.6
6.	Membership of House of Representatives at each apportionment[7]	. . .	. . .	. . .	. . .	1	3	4	6	9
7.	White population[8, 9, 10]	. . .	. . .	4,618	8,722	31,346	211,560	395,071	736,142	1,167,282
8.	Percent increase in white population over preceding census[9, 10, 11]	. . .	. . .	. . .	88.9	259.4	574.9	86.7	86.3	58.6
9.	Negro population[8, 9, 10]	. . .	. . .	144	174	293	707	2,583	6,799	11,849
10.	Percentage increase in Negro population over preceding census[9, 10, 11, 12, 13]	. . .	. . .	. . .	20.8	68.4	141.3	265.3	163.2	74.3
11.	Percent Negro in total population[1, 8, 9, 10, 14, 15]	. . .	. . .	3.0	2.0	0.9	0.3	0.7	0.9	1.0
12.	Number of slaves in the area enumerated in 1790 and in the added area[16]	. . .	. . .	24	. . .	1	. . .	. . .	. . .	. . .
13.	Urban population[17]	. . .	. . .	. . .	. . .	. . .	9,102	29,025	99,701	237,985
14.	Percent urban increase[17]	. . .	. . .	. . .	. . .	. . .	. . .218	.9	243.5	138.7
15.	Rural population[17]	. . .	. . .	4,762	8,896	31,639	203,165	368,629	649,412	946,074
16.	Percent rural increase over preceding census[17]	. . .	. . .	. . .	86.8	255.7	542.1	81.4	76.2	45.7
17.	Percent of urban to total population[17]	. . .	. . .	. . .	. . .	. . .	4.3	7.3	13.3	20.1
18.	Percent of rural to total population[17]	. . .	. . .	100.0	100.0	100.0	95.7	92.7	86.7	79.9
19.	Number of farms[18, 19]	. . .	. . .	. . .	. . .	. . .	. . .	34,089	62,422	98,786
20.	Acres in farms[18, 19]	. . .	. . .	. . .	. . .	. . .	. . .	4,383,890	7,030,834	10,019,142
21.	Acres improved land in farms[20]	. . .	. . .	. . .	. . .	. . .	. . .	1,929,110	3,476,296	5,096,939
22.	Cropland harvested, acres[18, 19]	. . .	. . .	. . .	. . .	. . .	. . .	NA	NA	NA
23.	Percentage increase in number of farms[18, 19]	. . .	. . .	. . .	. . .	. . .	. . .	. . .	83.1	58.3
24.	Percentage increase of land in farms[18, 19]	. . .	. . .	. . .	. . .	. . .	. . .	. . .	60.4	42.5
25.	Percentage increase of improved land in farms[20]	. . .	. . .	. . .	. . .	. . .	. . .	. . .	80.2	46.6

General Population, Agriculture, and Manufacturing Statistics, 1790-1970

MICHIGAN

1880	1890	1900	1910	1920	1930	1940	1950	1960	1970
1,636,937	2,093,890	2,420,982	2,810,173	3,668,412	4,842,325	5,256,106	6,371,766	7,823,194	8,875,083
38.2	27.9	15.6	16.1	30.5	32.0	8.5	21.2	22.8	13.4
452,878	456,952	327,093	389,191	858,239	1,173,912	413,781	1,115,660	1,451,428	1,051,889
3.3	3.3	3.2	3.0	3.5	3.9	4.0	4.2	4.4	4.4
28.5	36.4	42.1	48.9	63.8	84.9	92.2	111.7	137.7	156.2
11	12	12	13	13	17	17	18	19	19
1,614,560	2,072,884	2,398,563	2,785,247	3,601,627	4,663,507	5,039,643	5,917,825	7,085,865	7,833,474
38.3	28.4	15.7	16.1	29.3	29.4	8.1	17.4	19.7	10.6
15,100	15,223	15,816	17,115	60,082	169,453	208,345	442,296	717,581	991,066
27.4	0.8	3.9	8.2	251.0	182.0	23.0	112.3	62.2	38.1
0.9	0.7	0.7	0.6	1.6	3.5	4.0	6.9	9.2	11.2
. . .	. . .	. . .	. . .	. . .	. . .	. . .	. . .	. . .	. . .
405,412	730,294	952,323	1,327,044	2,241,560	3,302,075	3,454,867	4,166,165[c] / 4,503,084[d]	5,085,882[c] / 5,739,132[d]	6,553,773[d]
70.4	80.1	30.4	39.3	68.9	47.3	4.6	20.6[c]	22.1[c] / 27.4[d]	14.2[d]
1,231,525	1,363,596	1,468,659	1,483,129	1,426,852	1,540,250	1,801,239	2,205,601[c] / 1,868,682[d]	2,737,312[c] / 2,084,062[d]	2,321,310[d]
30.2	10.7	7.7	1.0	-3.8	7.9	16.9	22.4[c]	24.1[c] / 11.5[d]	11.4[d]
24.8	34.9	39.3	47.2	61.1	68.2	65.7	65.4[c] / 70.7[d]	65.0[c] / 73.4[d]	73.8[d]
75.2	65.1	60.7	52.8	38.9	31.8	34.3	34.6[c] / 29.3[d]	35.0[c] / 26.6[d]	26.2[d]
154,008	172,344	203,261	206,960	196,447	169,372	187,589	155,589	111,817	77,946
13,807,240	14,785,636	17,561,698	18,940,614	19,032,961	17,118,951	18,037,995	17,269,992	14,782,507	11,900,689
8,296,862	9,865,350	11,799,250	12,832,078	12,925,521	. . .	. . .	. . .	. . .	. . .
4,764,811	6,116,504	7,741,175	8,198,578	9,169,921	7,738,221	7,862,858	7,797,346	7,154,811	5,501,729
55.9	11.9	17.9	1.8	-5.1	-11.9	-4.5	-11.2	-19.5	-30.3
37.8	7.1	18.8	7.9	0.5	-5.1	-2.3	-6.1	-10.2	-19.5
62.8	18.9	19.6	8.8	0.7	. . .	. . .	. . .	. . .	. . .

General Population, Agriculture, and Manufacturing Statistics, 1790-1970—MICHIGAN (Cont.)

Item No.		1790 (or 1789)	1800	1810	1820	1830	1840	1850	1860	1870
26.	Average acreage per farm[18, 19]	. . .	. . .	. . .	. . .	. . .	. . .	128.6	112.6	101.4
27.	Percentage increase in cropland harvested[18, 19]	. . .	. . .	. . .	. . .	. . .	. . .	. . .	. . .	. . .
28.	Value of farms, dollars[18, 19]	. . .	. . .	. . .	. . .	. . .	. . .	51,872,446	160,836,495	318,592,463
29.	Value of farms, percent increase[18, 19]	. . .	. . .	. . .	. . .	. . .	. . .	. . .	210.1	98.1
30.	Average value per farm, dollars[18, 19]	. . .	. . .	. . .	. . .	. . .	. . .	1,522	2,577	3,225
31.	Farms operated by owners[21, 22, 23, 24, 25, 26, 27]	. . .	. . .	. . .	. . .	. . .	. . .	. . .	. . .	. . .
32.	Value of livestock on farms, dollars[28, 29, 30, 36]	. . .	. . .	. . .	. . .	. . .	. . .	8,008,734	23,714,771	39,847,895[b]
33.	Average value of livestock per farm, dollars[19, 28, 29, 30, 36]	. . .	. . .	. . .	. . .	. . .	. . .	235	380	403[b]
34.	Production of wheat in bushels[31, 32, 35, 36]	. . .	. . .	. . .	. . .	. . .	2,157,108	4,925,889	8,336,358	16,265,773
35.	Percent of total production of wheat[31, 32, 33, 35, 36]	. . .	. . .	. . .	. . .	. . .	2.5	4.9	4.8	5.6
36.	Production of corn in bushels[36, 37, 38, 39]	. . .	. . .	. . .	. . .	. . .	. . .	5,641,420	12,444,676	14,086,238
37.	Percent of total production of corn[36, 37, 38, 39]	. . .	. . .	. . .	. . .	. . .	. . .	1.0	1.5	1.9
38.	Production of oats in bushels[31, 35, 36]	. . .	. . .	. . .	. . .	. . .	2,114,051	2,866,056	4,036,980	8,954,466
39.	Percent of total production of oats[31, 35, 36]	. . .	. . .	. . .	. . .	. . .	1.7	1.9	2.3	3.2
40.	Production of soybeans in bushels[36, 40, 41]	. . .	. . .	. . .	. . .	. . .	. . .	. . .	. . .	. . .
41.	Percent of total production of soybeans[36, 40, 41]	. . .	. . .	. . .	. . .	. . .	. . .	. . .	. . .	. . .
42.	Production of hay crops in tons[31, 34, 42, 43, 44]	. . .	. . .	. . .	. . .	. . .	130,805	404,934	768,256	1,290,923
43.	Percent of total production of hay crops[31, 34, 42, 43, 44]	. . .	. . .	. . .	. . .	. . .	1.3	2.9	4.0	4.7
44.	Number of manufacturing establishments[44, 46, 47, 48]	. . .	. . .	. . .	. . .	. . .	. . .	2,033	3,448	9,455
45.	Capital of manufacturing establishments[45, 46, 47, 48]	. . .	. . .	. . .	. . .	. . .	. . .	6,563,660	23,808,226	71,712,283
46.	Average number of wage earners[45, 46, 47, 48]	. . .	. . .	. . .	. . .	. . .	. . .	9,344	23,190	63,694
47.	Total wages[45, 46, 47, 48]	. . .	. . .	. . .	. . .	. . .	. . .	2,717,124	6,735,047	21,205,355
48.	Cost of materials used in manufacturing[45, 46, 47, 48]	. . .	. . .	. . .	. . .	. . .	. . .	6,136,328	17,635,611	68,142,515
49.	Value of manufactured product[45, 46, 47, 48]	. . .	. . .	. . .	. . .	. . .	. . .	11,169,002	32,658,356	118,394,676

b. Values in gold

c. Previous urban definition

d. Present urban definition

1880	1890	1900	1910	1920	1930	1940	1950	1960	1970
89.7	85.8	86.4	91.5	96.9	101.1	96.2	111.0	132.2	152.7
NA	28.4	26.6	5.9	11.8	-9.0	-5.9	-8.5	-6.6	-23.1
499,103,181	556,190,670	582,517,710	901,138,299	1,436,686,210	1,160,651,607	912,545,223	1,701,440,000	2,855,261,000	3,883,355,000
56.7	11.4	4.7	54.7	59.4	-9.6	10.4	41.9	30.1	36.0
3,241	3,227	2,866	4,354	7,313	6,853	4,865	10,935	25,535	49,821
138,597	148,208	171,048	172,310	159,406	141,647	154,928	141,145	103,594	73,698
55,720,113	69,564,985	79,042,644	137,803,795	203,394,850	162,105,215	136,685,230	262,833,558	297,330,001	308,280,000
362	404	389	666	1,040	957	729	1,689	2,659	3,955
35,532,543	24,771,171	20,535,140	16,025,791	20,411,825	13,711,136	15,804,411	29,666,000	34,597,340	22,035,000
7.7	5.3	3.1	2.3	2.2	1.7	2.2	2.9	3.3	1.6
32,461,452	28,785,579	44,584,130	52,906,842	45,088,912	15,635,217	47,287,199	64,393,111	121,240,000	114,076,000
1.8	1.4	1.7	2.1	1.9	0.7	2.0	2.3	2.8	2.8
18,190,793	36,961,193	36,338,145	43,869,502	36,956,425	33,523,336	41,102,609	44,870,017	36,282,364	27,086,000
4.5	4.6	3.9	4.4	3.5	3.4	4.7	3.9	3.6	3.0
. . .	. . .	. . .	. . .	. . .	13,251	824,505	1,279,178	5,417,149	13,624,000
. . .	. . .	. . .	. . .	. . .	. . .	0.9	0.6	1.0	1.2
1,393,845	2,385,155	2,703,214	3,632,939	3,172,012	3,495,495	3,378,166	2,868,700	3,477,938	3,260,000
4.0	3.6	3.64	3.7	3.5	4.1	4.1	3.2	3.3	2.6
8,873	12,127	16,807	9,159	8,305	6,686	6,311			
92,930,959	262,412,240	284,097,133	583,947,000	2,340,954,000					
77,591	148,674	162,355	231,499	471,242	530,035	522,242		See following tables	
25,313,682	54,982,906	66,467,867	118,968,000	639,708,000	840,505,000	789,976,000			
92,900,269	154,521,918	199,559,905	368,612,000	1,919,243,000	2,589,374,000	2,549,819,000			
150,715,025	277,896,706	356,944,082	685,109,000	3,466,188,000	4,656,718,000	4,348,223,000			

General Population, Agriculture, and Manufacturing Statistics, 1790-1970

MINNESOTA

Item No.		1790 (or 1789)	1800	1810	1820	1830	1840	1850	1860	187
1.	Population[1]	...	...	...	...	...	...	6,077	172,023	439,706
2.	Decennial rates of increase in population over preceding census[2]	...	...	...	...	...	...	...	1,000+	155.6
3.	Increase in population over previous census[1, 3]	...	...	...	...	...	...	6,077	165,946	267,683
4.	Percent distribution of population[4]	...	...	...	...	...	...	...	0.5	1.1
5.	Population per square mile of land area[5, 6]	...	...	...	...	...	...	...	2.1	5.4
6.	Membership of House of Representatives at each apportionment[7]	...	...	...	...	...	...	2	2	3
7.	White population[8, 9, 10]	...	...	...	...	...	...	6,038	169,395	438,257
8.	Percent increase in white population over preceding census[9, 10, 11]	...	...	...	...	...	...	...	2,705.5	158.7
9.	Negro population[8, 9, 10]	...	...	...	...	...	...	39	259	759
10.	Percentage increase in Negro population over preceding census[9, 10, 11, 12, 13, 14]	...	...	...	...	...	...	...	564.1	193.1
11.	Percent Negro in total population[1, 8, 9, 10, 14, 15]	...	...	...	...	...	...	...	0.6	0.2
12.	Number of slaves in the area enumerated in 1790 and in the added area[16]	...	...	...	...	...	...	...	...	...
13.	Urban population[17]	...	...	...	...	...	...	...	16,223	70,754
14.	Percent urban increase[17]	...	...	...	...	...	...	...	...	336.1
15.	Rural population[17]	...	...	...	...	...	...	6,077	155,800	368,952
16.	Percent rural increase over preceding census[17]	...	...	...	...	...	...	...	1,000+	136.8
17.	Percent of urban to total population[17]	...	...	...	...	...	...	...	9.4	16.1
18.	Percent of rural to total population[17]	...	...	...	...	...	...	100.0	90.6	83.9
19.	Number of farms[18, 19]	...	...	...	...	...	...	157	18,181	46,500
20.	Acres in farms[18, 19]	...	...	...	...	...	...	28,881	2,711,968	6,483,828
21.	Acres improved land in farms[20]	...	...	...	...	...	...	5,035	556,250	2,322,102
22.	Cropland harvested, acres[18, 19]	...	...	...	...	...	...	...	...	NA
23.	Percentage increase in number of farms[18, 19]	...	...	...	...	...	...	...	...	155.8
24.	Percentage increase of land in farms[18, 19]	...	...	...	...	...	...	...	...	139.1
25.	Percentage increase of improved land in farms[20]	...	...	...	...	...	...	...	...	317.4

General Population, Agriculture, and Manufacturing Statistics, 1790-1970

MINNESOTA

1880	1890	1900	1910	1920	1930	1940	1950	1960	1970
780,773	1,310,283	1,751,394	2,075,708	2,387,125	2,563,953	2,792,300	2,982,483	3,413,864	3,804,971
77.6	67.8	33.7	18.5	15.0	7.4	8.9	6.8	14.5	11.5
341,067	521,053	440,160	324,314	311,417	176,828	228,347	190,183	431,381	391,107
1.6	2.1	2.3	2.3	2.3	2.1	2.1	2.0	1.9	1.9
9.7	16.2	21.7	25.7	29.5	32.0	34.9	37.3	43.1	48.0
5	7	9	10	10	9	9	9	8	8
776,884	1,296,408	1,737,036	2,059,227	2,368,936	2,542,599	2,768,982	2,953,697	3,371,603	3,736,038
77.3	66.9	34.0	18.5	15.0	7.3	8.9	6.7	14.1	10.8
1,564	3,683	4,959	7,084	8,809	9,445	9,928	14,022	22,263	34,868
106.1	135.5	34.6	42.9	24.4	7.2	5.1	41.2	58.8	56.6
0.2	0.3	0.3	0.3	0.4	0.4	0.4	0.5	0.6	0.9
. . .	. . .	. . .	. . .	. . .	. . .	. . .	. . .	. . .	. . .
148,758	443,049	598,100	850,294	1,051,593	1,257,616	1,390,098	1,607,446[c] / 1,624,914[d]	2,081,140[c] / 2,122,566[d]	2,527,308[d]
110.2	197.8	35.0	42.2	23.7	19.6	10.5	15.6[c]	29.5[c] / 30.6[d]	19.1[d]
632,015	867,234	1,153,294	1,225,414	1,335,532	1,306,337	1,402,202	1,375,037[c] / 1,357,569[d]	1,332,724[c] / 1,291,298[d]	1,277,663[d]
71.3	37.2	33.0	6.3	9.0	-2.2	7.3	-1.9[c]	-3.1[c] / -4.9[d]	-1.1[d]
19.1	33.8	34.1	41.0	44.1	49.0	49.8	53.9[c] / 54.5[d]	61.0[c] / 62.2[d]	66.4[d]
80.9	66.2	65.9	59.0	55.9	51.0	50.2	46.1[c] / 45.5[d]	39.0[c] / 37.8[d]	33.6[d]
92,386	116,851	154,659	156,137	178,478	185,255	197,351	179,101	145,662	110,747
13,403,019	18,663,645	26,248,498	27,675,823	30,221,758	30,913,367	32,606,962	32,883,163	30,796,097	28,845,240
7,246,693	11,127,953	18,442,585	19,643,533	21,481,710	. . .	. . .			
5,287,758	9,419,785	15,119,570	14,731,464	16,364,914	18,445,306	18,807,114	19,709,121	18,917,911	15,649,057
98.7	26.5	32.4	1.0	14.3	-1.6	-2.9	-5.2	-11.8	-24.0
106.7	39.2	40.6	5.4	9.2	2.8	-0.6	-0.8	-4.6	-6.3
212.1	53.6	65.7	6.5	9.4					

General Population, Agriculture, and Manufacturing Statistics, 1790-1970—MINNESOTA (Cont.)

Item No.	1790 (or 1789)	1800	1810	1820	1830	1840	1850	1860	1870
26. Average acreage per farm[18, 19]	...	...	...	...	...	...	183.9	149.2	139.4
27. Percentage increase in cropland harvested[18, 19]	...	...	...	...	...	...	...	NA	NA
28. Value of farms, dollars[18, 19]	...	...	...	...	...	...	161,948	27,505,922	78,277,954
29. Value of farms, percent increase[18, 19]	...	...	...	...	...	...	...	...	184.6
30. Average value per farm, dollars[18, 19]	...	...	...	...	...	...	1,032	1,513	1,683
31. Farms operated by owners[21, 22, 23, 24, 25, 26, 27]	...	...	...	...	...	...	...	...	...
32. Value of livestock on farms, dollars[28, 29, 30, 36]	...	...	...	...	...	...	92,859	3,642,841	16,095,073[b]
33. Average value of livestock per farm, dollars[19, 28, 29, 30, 36]	...	...	...	...	...	...	591	200	346[b]
34. Production of wheat in bushels[31, 32, 35, 36]	...	...	...	...	...	...	1,401	2,186,993	18,866,073
35. Percent of total production of wheat[31, 32, 33, 35, 36]	...	...	...	...	...	...	a	1.3	6.6
36. Production of corn in bushels[36, 37, 38, 39]	...	...	...	...	...	...	16,725	2,941,952	4,743,117
37. Percent of total production of corn[36, 37, 38, 39]	...	...	...	...	...	...	a	0.3	0.6
38. Production of oats in bushels[31, 35, 36]	...	...	...	...	...	...	30,582	2,176,002	10,678,261
39. Percent of total production of oats[31, 35, 36]	...	...	...	...	...	...	a	1.3	3.8
40. Production of soybeans in bushels[36, 40, 41]	...	...	...	...	...	...	...	...	...
41. Percent of total production of soybeans[36, 40, 41]	...	...	...	...	...	...	...	...	...
42. Production of hay crops in tons[31, 34, 42, 43]	...	...	...	...	...	...	2,019	179,482	695,053
43. Percent of total production of hay crops[31, 34, 42, 43, 44]	...	...	...	...	...	...	a	0.9	2.6
44. Number of manufacturing establishments[45, 46, 47, 48]	...	...	...	...	...	...	5	562	2,270
45. Capital of manufacturing establishments[45, 46, 47, 48]	...	...	...	...	...	...	94,000	2,388,310	11,993,729
46. Average number of wage earners[45, 46, 47, 48]	...	...	...	...	...	...	63	2,123	11,290
47. Total wages[45, 46, 47, 48]	...	...	...	...	...	...	18,540	712,214	4,052,837
48. Cost of materials used in manufacturing[45, 46, 47, 48]	...	...	...	...	...	...	24,300	1,904,070	13,842,902
49. Value of manufactured product[45, 46, 47, 48]	...	...	...	...	...	...	58,300	3,373,172	23,110,700

a. Less than 0.1%

b. Values in gold

c. Previous urban definition

d. Present urban definition

1880	1890	1900	1910	1920	1930	1940	1950	1960	1970
145.1	159.7	169.7	177.3	169.3	166.9	165.2	183.6	211.4	260.5
NA	78.1	60.5	-2.6	11.1	2.9	9.6	6.2	-2.9	-17.3
193,724,260	340,059,470	669,522,315	1,262,441,426	3,301,168,325	2,125,093,278	1,443,021,290	2,777,312,000	4,749,296,000	6,512,325,000
147.5	75.5	96.9	88.6	161.5	-11.2	4.3	51.5	36.5	37.1
2,097	2,910	4,329	8,085	18,496	11,471	7,312	15,507	32,605	58,803
83,933	101,747	127,904	122,104	132,744	126,570	132,903	141,330	119,294	97,827
31,904,821	57,725,683	89,063,097	161,641,146	304,245,296	300,970,571	227,946,324	535,226,163	652,645,858	791,600,000
345	494	576	1,035	1,704	1,624	1,155	2,988	4,481	7,148
34,601,030	52,300,247	95,278,650	57,094,412	37,616,384	19,760,092	20,341,862	15,512,000	21,535,651	22,882,000
7.5	11.2	14.5	8.3	4.0	2.5	2.9	1.5	2.0	1.7
14,831,741	24,696,446	47,256,920	67,897,051	84,786,096	104,419,048	162,766,107	207,669,742	339,913,000	390,490,000
0.8	1.2	1.8	2.7	3.6	4.9	7.0	7.5	7.9	9.5
23,382,158	49,958,791	74,054,150	93,897,717	89,108,151	126,221,063	143,070,552	165,008,851	157,080,385	167,700,000
5.7	6.2	7.8	9.3	8.4	12.7	16.4	14.5	15.7	18.4
. . .	. . .	. . .	. . .	. . .	3,380	466,585	12,912,013	41,379,627	82,124,000
. . .	. . .	. . .	. . .	. . .	. . .b	0.5	6.0	8.0	7.3
1,637,109	3,135,241	4,226,828	5,631,168	5,665,616	5,549,722	6,131,243	5,094,940	6,404,474	8,155,000
4.7	4.7	5.9	6.5	6.2	6.5	7.4	5.7	6.0	6.4
3,493	7,505	11,114	5,561	6,225	4,315	4,008			
31,004,811	127,686,618	165,832,246	275,416,000	679,386,000	. . .	. . .			
21,247	69,790	77,234	84,767	115,623	103,414	79,753			
8,613,094	30,371,123	35,484,825	47,471,000	127,107,000	132,418,000	96,887,000			
55,660,681	118,481,941	173,425,615	281,622,000	883,090,000	768,218,000	535,143,000			
76,065,198	192,033,478	262,655,881	409,420,000	1,218,120,000	1,173,214,000	845,772,000			

} See following tables

MISSOURI

Item No.		1790 (or 1789)	1800	1810	1820	1830	1840	1850	1860	1870
1.	Population[1]	...	...	19,783	66,586	140,455	383,702	682,044	1,182,012	1,721,295
2.	Decennial rates of increase in population over preceding census[2]	...	...	...	236.6	110.9	173.2	77.8	73.3	45.0
3.	Increase in population over previous census[1, 3]	...	...	20,845	45,741	73,869	243,247	298,342	499,968	539,283
4.	Percent distribution of population[4]	...	...	0.3	0.7	1.1	2 .2	2.9	3.8	4.5
5.	Population per square mile of land area[5, 6]	...	...	...	...	...	...	9.9	17.2	25.0
6.	Membership of House of Representatives at each apportionment[7]	...	...	...	1	2	5	7	9	13
7.	White population[8, 9, 10]	...	...	17,227	56,017	114,795	323,888	592,004	1,063,489	1,603,146
8.	Percent increase in white population over preceding census[9, 10, 11]	...	...	...	225.2	104.9	182.1	82.8	79.6	50.1
9.	Negro population[8, 9, 10]	...	...	3,618	10,569	25,660	59,814	90,040	118,503	118,071
10.	Percentage increase in Negro population over preceding census[9, 10, 11, 12, 13]	...	...	...	192.1	142.8	133.1	50.5	31.6	-0.4
11.	Percent Negro in total population[1, 8, 9, 10, 14, 15]	...	...	18.3	15.9	18.3	15.6	13.2	10.0	6.9
12.	Number of slaves in the area enumerated in 1790 and in the added area[16]	...	...	2,875	10,222	25,091	58,240	87,422	114,931	...
13.	Urban population[17]	...	...	...	...	4,977	16,469	80,558	203,487	429,578
14.	Percent urban increase[17]	...	...	...	...	...	230.9	389.1	152.6	111.1
15.	Rural population[17]	...	...	19,783	66,586	135,478	367,233	601,486	978,525	1,291,717
16.	Percent rural increase over preceding census[17]	...	...	...	236.6	103.5	171.1	63.8	62.7	32.0
17.	Percent of urban to total population[17]	...	...	...	...	3.5	4.3	11.8	17.2	25.0
18.	Percent of rural to total population[17]	...	...	100.0	100.0	96.5	95.7	88.2	82.8	75.0
19.	Number of farms[18, 19]	...	...	...	...	...	...	54,458	92,792	148,328
20.	Acres in farms[18, 19]	...	...	...	...	...	...	9,732,670	19,984,810	21,707,220
21.	Acres improved land in farms[20]	...	...	...	...	...	...	2,938,425	6,246,871	9,130,615
22.	Cropland harvested, acres[18, 19]	...	...	...	...	...	...	NA	NA	NA
23.	Percentage increase in number of farms[18, 19]	...	...	...	...	...	...	...	70.4	59.8
24.	Percentage increase of land in farms[18, 19]	...	...	...	...	...	...	...	105.3	8.6
25.	Percentage increase of improved land in farms[20]	...	...	...	...	...	...	...	112.6	46.2

MISSOURI

1880	1890	1900	1910	1920	1930	1940	1950	1960	1970
2,168,380	2,679,185	3,106,665	3,293,335	3,404,055	3,629,367	3,784,664	3,954,653	4,319,813	4,676,501
26.0	23.6	16.0	6.0	3.4	6.6	4.3	4.5	9.2	8.3
447,085	510,804	427,481	186,670	110,720	225,312	155,297	169,989	365,160	356,688
4.3	4.3	4.1	3.6	3.2	2.9	2.9	2.6	2.4	2.3
31.6	39.0	45.2	47.9	49.5	52.4	54.6	57.1	62.6	67.8
14	15	16	16	16	13	13	11	10	10
2,022,826	2,528,458	2,944,843	3,134,932	3,225,044	3,403,876	3,539,187	3,655,593	3,922,967	4,177,495
26.2	25.0	16.5	6.5	2.9	5.5	3.9	3.3	7.3	6.5
145,350	150,184	161,234	157,452	178,241	223,840	244,386	297,088	390,853	480,172
23.1	3.3	7.4	-2.3	13.2	25.6	9.2	2.2	3.2	2.3
6.7	5.6	5.2	4.8	5.2	6.2	6.5	7.5	9.0	10.3
. . .	. . .	. . .	. . .	. . .	. . .	. . .	. . .	. . .	. . .
545,993	856,966	1,128,104	1,393,705	1,586,903	1,859,119	1,960,696	2,290,149[c] 2,432,715[d]	2,647,003[c] 2,876,557[d]	3,277,662[d]
27.1	57.0	31.6	23.5	13.9	17.2	5.5	16.8[c]	15.6[c] 18.2[d]	13.9[d]
1,622,387	1,822,219	1,978,561	1,899,630	1,817,152	1,770,248	1,823,968	1,664,504[c] 521,938[d]	1,672,810[c] 1,443,256[d]	1,398,839[d]
25.6	12.3	8.6	-4.0	-4.3	-2.6	3.0	-8.7[c]	0.5[c] -5.2[d]	-3.1[d]
25.2	32.0	36.3	42.3	46.6	51.2	51.8	57.9[c] 61.5[d]	61.3[c] 66.6[d]	70.1[d]
74.8	68.0	63.7	57.7	53.4	48.8	48.2	42.1[c] 38.5[d]	38.7[c] 33.4[d]	29.9[d]
215,575	238,043	284,886	277,244	263,004	255,940	256,100	230,045	168,672	137,067
27,879,276	30,780,290	33,997,873	34,591,248	34,774,679	33,745,019	34,739,598	35,123,143	33,155,226	32,420,284
16,745,031	19,792,313	22,900,043	24,581,186	24,832,966	. . .	. . .	. . .	. . .	. . .
10,041,817	12,861,453	14,351,177	14,335,588	15,419,907	13,175,947	12,399,860	12,263,847	12,177,822	10,035,742
45.3	10.4	19.7	-2.7	-5.1	-1.7	-8.0	-5.3	-16.3	-18.7
28.4	10.4	10.5	1.7	0.5	3.4	-0.9	-0.4	-3.0	-2.2
83.4	18.2	15.7	7.3	1.0	. . .	. . .	. . .	. . .	. . .

General Population, Agriculture, and Manufacturing Statistics, 1790-1970—MISSOURI (Cont.)

Item No.		1790 (or 1789)	1800	1810	1820	1830	1840	1850	1860	1870
26.	Average acreage per farm[18, 19]	...	...	...	...	...	...	178.7	215.4	146.3
27.	Percentage increase in cropland harvested[18, 19]	...	...	...	...	...	...	...	NA	NA
28.	Value of farms, dollars[18, 19]	...	...	...	...	...	...	63,225,543	230,632,126	314,326,438
29.	Value of farms, percent increase[18, 19]	...	...	...	...	...	...	...	264.8	36.3
30.	Average value per farm, dollars[18, 19]	...	...	...	...	...	...	1,161	2,485	2,119
31.	Farms operated by owners[21, 22, 23, 24, 25, 26, 27]	...	...	...	...	...	...	...	...	...
32.	Value of livestock on farms, dollars[28, 29, 30, 36]	...	...	...	...	...	...	19,887,580	53,693,673	67,428,218[b]
33.	Average value of livestock per farm, dollars[19, 28, 29, 30, 36]	...	...	...	...	...	...	365	579	455[b]
34.	Production of wheat in bushels[31, 32, 35, 36]	...	...	...	...	...	1,037,386	2,981,652	4,227,586	14,315,926
35.	Percent of total production of wheat[31, 32, 33, 35, 36]	...	...	...	...	...	1.2	3.0	2.4	5.0
36.	Production of corn in bushels[36, 37, 38, 39]	...	...	...	...	...	...	36,214,537	72,892,157	66,034,075
37.	Percent of total production of corn[36, 37, 38, 39]	...	...	...	...	...	...	6.1	8.7	8.7
38.	Production of oats in bushels[31, 35, 36]	...	...	...	...	...	2,234,947	5,278,079	3,680,870	16,578,313
39.	Percent of total production of oats[31, 35, 36]	...	...	...	...	...	1.8	3.6	2.1	5.9
40.	Production of soybeans in bushels[36, 40, 41]	...	...	...	...	...	...	...	...	...
41.	Percent of total production of soybeans[34, 36, 40, 41]	...	...	...	...	...	...	...	...	...
42.	Production of hay crops in tons[31, 34, 42, 43, 44]	...	...	...	...	...	49,083	116,925	401,070	615,611
43.	Percent of total production of hay crops[31, 34, 42, 43, 44]	...	...	...	...	...	...	0.9	2.1	2.3
44.	Number of manufacturing establishments[44, 46, 47, 48]	...	...	...	...	...	...	2,923	3,157	11,871
45.	Capital of manufacturing establishments[45, 46, 47, 48]	...	...	...	...	...	...	8,576,607	20,034,220	80,257,244
46.	Average number of wage earners[45, 46, 47, 48]	...	...	...	...	...	...	15,808	19,681	65,354
47.	Total wages[45, 46, 47, 48]	...	...	...	...	...	...	4,692,648	6,669,916	31,055,445
48.	Cost of materials used in manufacturing[45, 46, 47, 48]	...	...	...	...	...	...	12,798,351	23,849,941	115,533,269
49.	Value of manufactured product[45, 46, 47, 48]	...	...	...	...	...	...	24,324,418	41,782,731	206,213,429

b. Values in gold

c. Previous urban definition

d. Present urban definition

General Population, Agriculture, and Manufacturing Statistics, 1790-1970—MISSOURI (Cont.)

1880	1890	1900	1910	1920	1930	1940	1950	1960	1970
129.3	129.3	119.8	124.8	132.2	131.8	135.6	152.7	196.6	236.5
NA	28.1	11.6	-0.1	7.6	-4.0	5.4	-4.9	-1.5	-1.8
375,633,307	625,858,361	843,979,213	1,716,204,386	3,062,967,700	1,796,246,519	1,107,302,598	2,235,939,000	3,726,715,000	7,269,173,000
19.5	66.6	34.9	103.3	78.5	-10.3	0.7	46.4	33.8	95.1
1,742	2,629	2,963	6,190	11,646	7,018	4,324	9,720	22,094	53,034
156,703	174,285	197,989	192,285	185,030	165,318	163,763	183,101	143,855	124,270
95,785,282	138,701,173	160,540,004	285,839,108	387,201,999	257,955,342	188,775,965	493,729,253	606,400,133	839,800,000
444	583	564	1,031	1,482	1,008	737	2,146	3,595	6,127
24,966,627	30,113,821	23,072,768	29,837,429	65,210,462	15,116,509	30,890,536	23,782,000	35,731,219	31,222,000
5.4	6.4	3.5	4.4	6.9	1.9	4.4	2.3	3.4	2.8
202,414,413	196,999,016	208,844,870	191,427,087	146,342,036	112,348,071	124,058,341	129,968,135	232,485,000	173,057,000
11.5	9.3	7.8	7.5	6.2	5.3	5.4	4.7	5.4	4.2
20,670,958	39,820,149	20,545,350	24,828,501	40,493,700	19,050,770	34,771,104	30,223,572	15,645,290	9,184,000
5.1	4.9	2.2	2.5	3.8	1.9	4.0	2.7	1.6	1.0
...	...	...	...	...	725,114	1,090,829	16,738,422	47,441,259	88,358,000
...	...	...	...	...	8.4	12.4	7.9	9.2	7.9
1,083,929	3,567,635	3,907,508	3,816,836	3,358,316	3,564,805	3,259,443	4,392,710	3,882,963	5,535,000
3.1	5.3	5.5	4.4	3.7	4.2	3.9	4.9	3.6	4.3
8,592	14,052	18,754	8,375	8,592	5,765	4,796			
72,507,844	189,558,546	249,888,581	444,343,000	938,761,000	...	...		See following tables	
63,995	124,203	134,975	152,993	195,037	202,879	178,538			
24,309,716	59,643,429	60,719,428	80,843,000	196,515,000	240,369,000	190,736,000			
110,798,392	177,582,382	214,988,018	354,411,000	1,056,457,000	1,139,658,000	800,095,000			
165,386,205	324,561,993	385,492,784	574,111,000	1,594,208,000	1,917,155,000	1,388,056,000			

General Population, Agriculture, and Manufacturing Statistics, 1790-1970

NEBRASKA

Item No.		1790 (or 1789)	1800	1810	1820	1830	1840	1850	1860	1870
1.	Population[1]	...	...	...	...	...	...	...	28,841	122,993
2.	Decennial rates of increase in population over preceding census[2]		...	...	...	...	...	...	...	326.5
3.	Increase in population over previous census[1, 3]	...	...	...	...	...	...	...	28,841	94,152
4.	Percent distribution of population[4]	...	...	...	...	...	...	...	0.1	0.1
5.	Population per square mile of land area[5, 6]	...	...	...	...	...	...	...	0.2	1.6
6.	Membership of House of Representatives at each apportionment[7]	...	...	...	...	...	...	...	1	1
7.	White population[8, 9, 10]	...	...	...	...	...	...	...	28,696	122,117
8.	Percent increase in white population over preceding census[9, 10, 11]	...	...	...	...	...	...	...	...	325.6
9.	Negro population[8, 9, 10]	...	...	...	...	...	...	...	82	789
10.	Percentage increase in Negro population over preceding census[9, 10, 11, 12, 13, 14]	...	...	...	...	...	...	...	...	862.2
11.	Percent Negro in total population[1, 8, 9, 10, 14, 15]	...	...	...	...	...	...	...	0.3	0.6
12.	Number of slaves in the area enumerated in 1790 and in the added area[16]	...	...	...	...	...	...	...	15	...
13.	Urban population[17]	...	...	...	...	...	...	...	...	22,133
14.	Percent urban increase[17]	...	...	...	...	...	...	...	...	...
15.	Rural population[17]	...	...	...	...	...	...	...	28,841	100,860
16.	Percent rural increase over preceding census[17]	...	...	...	...	...	...	...	...	249.7
17.	Percent of urban to total population[17]	...	...	...	...	...	...	...	...	18.0
18.	Percent of rural to total population[17]	...	...	...	...	...	...	...	100.0	82.0
19.	Number of farms[18, 19]	...	...	...	...	...	...	...	2,789	12,301
20.	Acres in farms[18, 19]	...	...	...	...	...	...	...	631,214	2,073,781
21.	Acres improved land in farms[20]	...	...	...	...	...	...	...	118,789	647,031
22.	Cropland harvested, acres[18, 19]	...	...	...	...	...	...	...	...	...
23.	Percentage increase in number of farms[18, 19]	...	...	...	...	...	...	...	...	341.1
24.	Percentage increase of land in farms[18, 19]	...	...	...	...	...	...	...	...	228.5
25.	Percentage increase of improved land in farms[20]	...	...	...	...	...	...	...	...	444.7

General Population, Agriculture, and Manufacturing Statistics, 1790-1970

NEBRASKA

1880	1890	1900	1910	1920	1930	1940	1950	1960	1970
452,402	1,062,656	1,066,300	1,192,214	1,296,372	1,377,963	1,315,834	1,325,510	1,411,330	1,483,493
267.8	134.9	0.3	11.8	8.7	6.3	-4.5	0.7	6.5	5.1
329,409	606,508	7,390	125,914	104,158	81,591	-62,129	9,676	8,582	72,163
0.9	1.7	1.4	1.3	1.2	1.1	1.0	0.9	0.8	0.7
5.9	13.8	13.9	15.5	16.9	18.0	17.2	17.3	18.4	19.4
3	6	6	6	6	5	4	4	3	3
449,764	1,047,096	1,056,526	1,180,293	1,279,219	1,360,023	1,297,624	1,301,328	1,374,764	1,432,867
268.3	132.8	0.9	9.4	8.4	6.3	-4.6	0.2	5.6	-5.3
2,385	8,913	6,269	7,689	13,242	13,752	14,171	19,234	29,262	39,911
202.3	273.7	-29.7	22.6	72.2	3.9	3.0	3.6	52.1	36.4
0.5	0.8	0.6	0.6	1.0	1.0	1.1	1.5	2.1	2.7
. . .	. . .	. . .	. . .	. . .	. . .	. . .	. . .	. . .	. . .
61,307	291,641	252,702	310,852	405,293	486,107	514,148	606,530[c] 621,905[d]	733,595[c] 766,053[d]	912,598[d]
177.0	375.7	-13.4	23.0	30.4	19.9	5.8	18.0	20.9[c] 23.2[d]	19.1[d]
391,095	771,015	813,598	881,362	891,079	891,856	801,686	718,980[c] 703,605[d]	677,735[c] 645,277[d]	570,895[d]
287.8	97.1	5.5	8.3	1.1	0.1	-10.1	-10.3	-5.7[c] -8.3[d]	-11.5[d]
13.6	27.4	23.7	26.1	31.3	35.3	39.1	45.8[c] 46.9[d]	52.0[c] 54.3[d]	61.5[d]
86.4	72.6	76.3	73.9	68.7	64.7	60.9	54.2[c] 53.1[d]	48.0[c] 45.7[d]	38.5[d]
63,387	113,608	121,525	129,678	124,417	129,458	121,062	107,183	90,475	72,257
9,944,826	21,593,444	29,911,779	38,622,021	42,225,475	44,708,565	47,343,981	47,466,828	47,755,708	45,833,953
5,504,702	15,247,705	18,432,595	24,382,577	23,109,624	. . .	. . .	. . .	. . .	. . .
4,019,116	10,724,838	15,044,428	17,231,205	18,936,108	21,399,340	17,304,802	19,406,990	18,057,090	14,022,810
415.3	79.2	7.0	6.7	-4.1	1.3	-9.4	-4.1 -10.3	-20.1	
379.6	117.1	38.5	29.1	9.3	6.4	1.6	-0.6	0.6	-4.0
750.8	177.0	20.9	32.3	-5.2	. . .	. . .	. . .	. . .	. . .

General Population, Agriculture, and Manufacturing Statistics, 1790-1970—NEBRASKA (Cont.)

Item No.	1790 (or 1789)	1800	1810	1820	1830	1840	1850	1860	1870
26. Average acreage per farm[18, 19]	. . .	. . .	. . .	. . .	. . .	. . .	. . .	226.3	168.6
27. Percentage increase in cropland harvested[18, 19]	. . .	. . .	. . .	. . .	. . .	. . .	. . .	. . .	NA
28. Value of farms, dollars[18, 19]	. . .	. . .	. . .	. . .	. . .	. . .	. . .	3,878,326	24,193,749
29. Value of farms, percent increase[18, 19]	. . .	. . .	. . .	. . .	. . .	. . .	. . .	. . .	523.8
30. Average value per farm, dollars[18, 19]	. . .	. . .	. . .	. . .	. . .	. . .	. . .	1,391	1,967
31. Farms operated by owners[21, 22, 23, 24, 25, 26, 27]	. . .	. . .	. . .	. . .	. . .	. . .	. . .	. . .	. . .
32. Value of livestock on farms, dollars[28, 29, 30, 36]	. . .	. . .	. . .	. . .	. . .	. . .	. . .	1,128,771	5,240,948[b]
33. Average value of livestock per farm, dollars[19, 28, 29, 30, 36]	. . .	. . .	. . .	. . .	. . .	. . .	. . .	405	426[b]
34. Production of wheat in bushels[31, 32, 35, 36]	. . .	. . .	. . .	. . .	. . .	. . .	. . .	147,867	2,125,086
35. Percent of total production of wheat[31, 32, 33, 35, 36]	. . .	. . .	. . .	. . .	. . .	. . .	. . .	0.1	0.7
36. Production of corn in bushels[36, 37, 38, 39]	. . .	. . .	. . .	. . .	. . .	. . .	. . .	1,482,080	4,736,710
37. Percent of total production of corn[36, 37, 38, 39]	. . .	. . .	. . .	. . .	. . .	. . .	. . .	0.2	0.6
38. Production of oats in bushels[31, 35, 36]	. . .	. . .	. . .	. . .	. . .	. . .	. . .	74,502	1,477,562
39. Percent of total production of oats[31, 35, 36]	. . .	. . .	. . .	. . .	. . .	. . .	. . .	a	0.5
40. Production of soybeans in bushels[36, 40, 41]	. . .	. . .	. . .	. . .	. . .	. . .	. . .	. . .	. . .
41. Percent of total production of soybeans[36, 40, 41]	. . .	. . .	. . .	. . .	. . .	. . .	. . .	. . .	. . .
42. Production of hay crops in tons[31, 34, 42, 43, 44]	. . .	. . .	. . .	. . .	. . .	. . .	. . .	24,458	169,354
43. Percent of total production of hay crops[31, 34, 42, 43, 44]	. . .	. . .	. . .	. . .	. . .	. . .	. . .	0.1	0.6
44. Number of manufacturing establishments[45, 46, 47, 48]	. . .	. . .	. . .	. . .	. . .	. . .	. . .	107	670
45. Capital of manufacturing establishments[45, 46, 47, 48]	. . .	. . .	. . .	. . .	. . .	. . .	. . .	266,575	2,169,963
46. Average number of wage earners[45, 46, 47, 48]	. . .	. . .	. . .	. . .	. . .	. . .	. . .	336	2,665
47. Total wages[45, 46, 47, 48]	. . .	. . .	. . .	. . .	. . .	. . .	. . .	105,332	1,429,913
48. Cost of materials used in manufacturing[45, 46, 47, 48]	. . .	. . .	. . .	. . .	. . .	. . .	. . .	237,215	2,902,074
49. Value of manufactured product[45, 46, 47, 48]	. . .	. . .	. . .	. . .	. . .	. . .	. . .	607,328	5,738,512

a. Less than 0.1%
b. Values in gold
c. Previous urban definition
d. Present urban definition

General Population, Agriculture, and Manufacturing Statistics, 1790-1970—NEBRASKA (Cont.)

	1880	1890	1900	1910	1920	1930	1940	1950	1960	1970
	156.9	190.1	246.1	297.8	339.4	345.4	391.1	442.9	527.8	634.3
	NA	166.8	40.3	14.5	9.9	8.0	41.9	-1.0	-4.3	-22.3
	105,932,541	402,358,913	577,660,020	1,813,346,935	3,712,107,760	2,495,203,071	1,137,808,019	2,735,039,000	4,233,856,000	7,076,220,000
	337.9	279.8	43.6	213.9	104.7	-1.1	-27.2	61.0	24.5	67.1
	1,671	3,542	4,753	13,983	29,836	19,274	9,399	25,517	46,796	97,931
	51,963	85,525	76,715	79,250	69,672	67,418	56,561	65,103	58,617	54,503
	40,350,265	92,971,920	145,349,587	222,222,004	335,643,504	288,546,065	160,581,094	495,179,724	748,150,364	1,171,050,000
	637	818	1,196	1,714	2,704	2,229	1,326	4,620	8,269	16,207
	13,847,007	10,571,059	24,924,520	47,685,745	57,843,598	53,867,855	34,676,159	88,482,000	64,921,062	97,204,000
	3.0	2.3	3.8	7.0	6.1	6.7	4.9	8.7	6.1	7.1
	65,450,135	215,895,996	210,974,740	180,132,807	160,391,314	216,020,274	71,886,032	224,259,108	330,285,000	360,375,000
	3.7	10.2	7.9	7.1	6.8	10.1	3.1	8.0	7.7	8.8
	6,555,875	43,843,640	58,007,140	53,360,185	59,819,545	70,733,080	18,225,518	42,290,850	30,996,174	24,276,000
	1.6	5.4	6.1	5.3	5.7	7.1	2.1	3.7	3.1	2.7
	...	...	...	...	...	1,785	20,566	421,961	3,431,626	17,864,000
	...	...	...	...	...	a	a	0.2	6.7	1.5
	786,722	3,115,398	3,319,283	5,545,437	5,307,720	4,574,577	2,449,278	5,076,863	6,077,179	5,999,000
	2.2	4.7	4.7	6.4	4.8	5.4	3.0	5.7	5.7	4.7
	1,403	3,014	5,414	2,500	2,884	1,491	1,161			
	4,881,150	37,569,508	71,982,127	99,901,000	245,257,000	...	...			
	4,793	20,450	24,461	24,336	36,521	28,212	18,807		See following tables	
	1,742,311	10,271,478	11,570,688	13,948,000	46,067,000	36,881,000	20,624,000			
	8,208,478	67,334,532	102,197,707	151,081,000	480,774,000	364,175,000	204,437,000			
	12,627,336	93,037,794	143,990,102	199,019,000	596,042,000	484,168,000	273,525,000			

General Population, Agriculture, and Manufacturing Statistics, 1790-1970

North Dakota

Item No.		1790 (or 1789)	1800	1810	1820	1830	1840	1850	1860	1870
1.	Population[1]	...	...	...	...	...	...	...	4,837[a]	2,405
2.	Decennial rates of increase in population over preceding census[2]	...	...	...	...	...	...	...	...	193.1
3.	Increase in population over previous census[1, 3]	...	...	...	...	...	...	...	4,837[a]	9,344[a]
4.	Percent distribution of population[4]	...	...	...	...	...	...	...	...	...
5.	Population per square mile of land area[5, 6]	...	...	...	...	...	...	...	...	0.
6.	Membership of House of Representatives at each apportionment[7]	...	...	...	...	...	...	...	...	...
7.	White population[8, 9, 10]	...	...	...	...	...	...	...	2,576[a]	12,887[a]
8.	Percent increase in white population over preceding census[9, 10, 11]	...	...	...	...	...	...	...	...	400.3
9.	Negro population[8, 9, 10]	...	...	...	...	...	...	...	...	94[a]
10.	Percentage increase in Negro population over preceding census[9, 10, 11, 12, 13, 14]	...	...	...	...	...	...	...	...	...
11.	Percent Negro in total population[1, 8, 9, 10, 14, 15]	...	...	...	...	...	...	...	...	...
12.	Number of slaves in the area enumerated in 1790 and in the added area[16]	...	...	...	...	...	...	...	...	...
13.	Urban population[17]	...	...	...	...	...	...	...	...	...
14.	Percent urban increase[17]	...	...	...	...	...	...	...	...	...
15.	Rural population[17]	...	...	...	...	...	...	...	...	2,405[a]
16.	Percent rural increase over preceding census[17]	...	...	...	...	...	...	...	...	...
17.	Percent of urban to total population[17]	...	...	...	...	...	...	...	...	...
18.	Percent of rural to total population[17]	...	...	...	...	...	...	...	...	100.0
19.	Number of farms[18, 19]	...	...	...	...	...	...	...	123[a]	1,720[a]
20.	Acres in farms[18, 19]	...	...	...	...	...	...	...	26,448[a]	302,376[a]
21.	Acres improved land in farms[20]	...	...	...	...	...	...	...	2,115[a]	42,645[a]
22.	Cropland harvested, acres[18, 19]	...	...	...	...	...	...	...	NA	NA
23.	Percentage increase in number of farms[18, 19]	...	...	...	...	...	...	...	...	...
24.	Percentage increase of land in farms[18, 19]	...	...	...	...	...	...	...	...	...
25.	Percentage increase of improved land in farms[20]	...	...	...	...	...	...	...	...	...

General Population, Agriculture, and Manufacturing Statistics, 1790-1970

NORTH DAKOTA

1880	1890	1900	1910	1920	1930	1940	1950	1960	1970
36,909	190,983	319,146	577,056	646,872	680,845	641,935	619,636	632,446	617,761
1,434.7	417.4	67.1	80.8	12.1	5.3	-5.7	-3.5	2.1	-2.3
120,996	376,350	129,520	257,910	69,816	33,973	-38,910	-22,299	12,810	-14,685
0.1	0.3	0.4	0.6	0.6	0.6	0.5	0.4	0.4	0.3
0.9	2.7	4.5	8.2	9.2	9.7	9.2	8.8	9.1	8.9
1	1	2	3	3	2	2	2	2	1
36,192	182,407	311,712	569,855	639,954	671,851	631,464	608,448	619,538	599,485
933.2[a]	283.3[a]	70.9	82.8	12.3	5.0	-6.0	-3.6	0.2	-3.2
113[a]	373	286	617	467	377	201	257	777	2,494
326.6[a]	127.9[a]	-23.3	115.7	-24.3	-19.3	-46.7	27.9	202.3	221.0
0.3	0.2	0.1	0.1	0.1	0.1	e	e	0.1	4.0
. . .	. . .	. . .	. . .	. . .	. . .	. . .	. . .	. . .	. . .
2,693	10,643	23,413	63,236	88,239	113,306	131,923	164,817[c] / 164,817[d]	221,694[c] / 222,708[d]	273,442[d]
. . .	295.2	120.0	170.1	39.5	28.4	16.4	24.9[c]	34.5[c] / 35.1[d]	22.8[d]
34,216	180,340	295,733	513,820	558,633	567,539	510,012	454,819[c] / 454,819[d]	410,752[c] / 409,738[d]	344,319[d]
1,000+	427.1	64.0	73.7	8.7	1.6	-10.1	-10.8[c]	-9.7[c] / -9.9[d]	-16.0[d]
7.3	5.6	7.3	11.0	13.6	16.6	20.6	26.6[c] / 26.6[d]	35.1[c] / 35.2[d]	44.3[d]
92.7	94.4	92.7	89.0	86.4	83.4	79.4	73.4[c] / 73.4[d]	64.9[c] / 64.8[d]	55.7[d]
5,790	27,611	45,332	74,360	77,690	77,975	73,962	65,401	54,928	46,381
1,027,845	7,660,333	15,542,640	28,426,650	36,214,751	38,657,894	37,936,136	41,194,044	41,465,717	43,117,831
259,543	4,658,015	9,644,520	20,455,092	24,563,178	. . .	. . .	. . .	. . .	. . .
642,035	3,856,054	7,821,704	15,888,756	19,422,855	21,254,660	15,536,632	20,352,760	19,357,711	17,174,891
120.3	628.5	64.2	64.0	4.5	2.6	-12.6	-5.9	-11.3	-15.6
239.9	645.3	102.9	82.9	27.4	12.6	-3.0	0.5	-1.0	-4.0
508.6	. . .	107.1	112.1	20.1	. . .	. . .	. . .	. . .	. . .

General Population, Agriculture, and Manufacturing Statistics, 1790-1970—NORTH DAKOTA (Cont.)

Item No.	1790 (or 1789)	1800	1810	1820	1830	1840	1850	1860	1870
26. Average acreage per farm[18, 19]	...	...	...	...	...	...	...	215.0	175.8
27. Percentage increase in cropland harvested[18, 19]	...	...	...	...	...	...	...	NA	NA
28. Value of farms, dollars[18, 19]	...	...	...	...	...	...	...	96,445[a]	1,668,211[a]
29. Value of farms, percent increase[18, 19]	...	...	...	...	...	...	...	...	1,000+[a]
30. Average value per farm, dollars[18, 19]	...	...	...	...	...	...	...	784[a]	970[a]
31. Farms operated by owners[21, 22, 23, 24, 25, 26, 27]	...	...	...	...	...	...	...	...	...
32. Value of livestock on farms, dollars[28, 29, 30, 36]	...	...	...	...	...	...	...	39,116[a]	623,962[a,b]
33. Average value of livestock per farm, dollars[19, 28, 29, 30, 36]	...	...	...	...	...	...	...	318[a]	363[a,b]
34. Production of wheat in bushels[31, 32, 35, 36]	...	...	...	...	...	...	...	945[a]	170,662[a]
35. Percent of total production of wheat[31, 32, 35, 36]	...	...	...	...	...	...	...	e	e
36. Production of corn in bushels[36, 37, 38, 39]	...	...	...	...	...	...	...	20,269[a]	133,140[a]
37. Percent of total production of corn[36, 37, 38, 39]	...	...	...	...	...	...	...	e	e
38. Production of oats in bushels[31, 35, 36]	...	...	...	...	...	...	...	2,540[a]	114,327[a]
39. Percent of total production of oats[31, 35, 36]	...	...	...	...	...	...	...	e	e
40. Production of soybeans in bushels[36, 40, 41]	...	...	...	...	...	...	...	...	...
41. Percent of total production of soybeans[36, 40, 41]	...	...	...	...	...	...	...	...	...
42. Production of hay crops in tons[31, 34, 42, 43, 44]	...	...	...	...	...	...	...	855[a]	13,347[a]
43. Percent of total production of hay crops[31, 34, 42, 43, 44]	...	...	...	...	...	...	...	e	e
44. Number of manufacturing establishments[45, 46, 47, 48]	...	...	...	...	...	...	...	...	17[a]
45. Capital of manufacturing establishments[45, 46, 47, 48]	...	...	...	...	...	...	...	...	79,200[a]
46. Average number of wage earners[45, 46, 47, 48]	...	...	...	...	...	...	...	...	91[a]
47. Total wages[45, 46, 47, 48]	...	...	...	...	...	...	...	...	21,106[a]
48. Cost of materials used in manufacturing[45, 46, 47, 48]	...	...	...	...	...	...	...	...	105,997[a]
49. Value of manufactured product[45, 46, 47, 48]	...	...	...	...	...	...	...	...	178,570[a]

a. Dakota Territory (see f)

b. Values in gold

c. Previous urban definition

d. Present urban definition

e. Less than 0.1%

f. North Dakota and South Dakota admitted as States in 1889. Figures for 1879 obtained by consolidating data for the counties which then occupied the areas now known as North Dakota and South Dakota, respectively. The 1869 and 1859 figures are for Dakota Territory.

General Population, Agriculture, and Manufacturing Statistics, 1790-1970—NORTH DAKOTA (Cont.)

1880	1890	1900	1910	1920	1930	1940	1950	1960	1970
271.2	277.4	342.9	382.3	466.1	495.8	512.9	629.9	754.9	929.6
NA	500.6	102.8	103.1	22.2	6.9	66.2	-2.2	-8.9	-11.3
8,575,114	75,310,305	198,780,700	822,656,744	1,488,521,495	951,225,446	490,197,358	1,188,860,000	2,140,991,000	4,045,470,000
414.0	778.2	163.9	313.9	80.9	-6.8	-30.7	67.8	43.4	89.0
2,263	2,728	4,385	11,063	19,160	12,199	6,628	18,178	38,978	87,222
16,757	25,698	41,467	63,212	56,917	50,105	40,391	50,976	44,253	39,696
7,555,274	18,787,294	42,430,491	108,249,866	156,821,560	116,588,924	79,478,711	201,506,486	292,523,424	402,870,000
433	680	936	1,456	2,021	1,495	1,075	3,081	5,326	8,686
1,737,343[f]	26,403,365	59,888,810	116,781,886	61,540,404	95,574,408	69,261,286	123,986,000	94,798,822	152,826,000
0.4[f]	5.6	9.1	17.1	6.5	11.9	9.8	12.2	9.0	11.2
2,000,864[a]	178,729	1,284,870	4,941,152	3,876,883	2,172,643	6,630,344	11,465,677	22,126,000	6,500,000
0.1[a]	e	e	0.2	0.2	0.1	0.3	0.4	0.5	0.2
728,811[f]	5,773,129	22,125,331	65,886,702	30,294,074	31,174,936	33,104,454	32,220,244	39,116,923	115,541,000
0.2[f]	0.7	2.3	6.5	3.0	3.1	3.8	2.8	3.9	12.7
...	...	...	...	...	195	9,966	226,044	2,430,630	2,715,000
...	...	...	...	...	e	e	0.1	0.5	0.2
31,552[f]	531,472	1,719,274	2,902,351	2,929,651	2,362,585	2,392,734	2,901,939	2,968,110	4,414,000
0.1[f]	0.8	2.4	3.3	3.2	2.8	2.9	3.3	2.8	3.5
251[a]	382	1,130	752	894	373	350			
771,428[a]	2,894,553	5,396,490	11,585,000	24,550,000	...	...		See following table	
868[a]	1,499	2,398	2,789	4,472	4,024	2,637			
339,375[a]	759,132	1,222,472	1,787,000	5,401,000	5,687,000	2,771,000			
1,523,761[a]	3,087,161	5,615,793	13,674,000	44,489,000	39,684,000	32,665,000			
2,373,970[a]	5,028,107	9,183,114	19,137,000	57,374,000	55,322,000	43,767,000			

37

General Population, Agriculture, and Manufacturing Statistics, 1790-1970

OHIO

Item No.		1790 (or 1789)	1800	1810	1820	1830	1840	1850	1860	1870
1.	Population[1]	. . .	45,365	230,760	581,434	937,903	1,519,467	1,980,329	2,339,511	2,665,260
2.	Decennial rates of increase in population over preceding census[2]	. . .	. . .	408.7	152.0	61.3	62.0	30.3	18.1	13.9
3.	Increase in population over previous census[1, 3]	. . .	. . .	185,395	350,674	356,469	581,564	460,862	359,182	325,749
4.	Percent distribution of population[4]	. . .	0.9	3.2	6.0	7.3	8.9	8.9	7.4	6.9
5.	Population per square mile of land area[5, 6]	. . .	1.1	. . .	. . .	. . .	. . .	48.6	57.4	65.4
6.	Membership of House of Representatives at each apportionment[7]	. . .	1	6	14	19	21	21	19	20
7.	White population[8, 9, 10]	. . .	45,028	228,861	576,711	928,329	1,502,122	1,955,050	2,302,808	2,601,946
8.	Percent increase in white population over preceding census[9, 10, 11]	. . .	. . .	408.3	152.0	61.0	61.8	30.2	17.8	13.0
9.	Negro population[8, 9, 10]	. . .	337	1,899	4,723	9,574	17,345	25,279	36,673	63,213
10.	Percentage increase in Negro population over preceding census[9, 10, 11, 12, 13, 14]	. . .	. . .	463.5	148.7	102.7	81.2	45.7	45.1	72.4
11.	Percent Negro in total population[1, 8, 9, 10, 14, 15]	. . .	0.7	0.8	0.8	1.0	1.1	1.3	1.6	2.4
12.	Number of slaves in the area enumerated in 1790 and in the added area[16]	. . .	. . .	. . .	. . .	6	3	. . .	. . .	. . .
13.	Urban population[17]	. . .	. . .	2,540	9,642	36,658	83,491	242,418	400,435	682,922
14.	Percent urban increase[17]	. . .	. . .	. . .	279.6	280.2	127.8	190.4	65.2	70.5
15.	Rural population[17]	. . .	45,365	228,220	571,792	901,245	1,435,976	1,737,911	1,939,076	1,982,338
16.	Percent rural increase over preceding census[17]	. . .	. . .	403.1	150.5	57.6	59.3	21.0	11.6	2.2
17.	Percent of urban to total population[17]	. . .	. . .	1.1	1.7	3.9	5.5	12.2	17.1	25.6
18.	Percent of rural to total population[17]	. . .	100.0	98.9	98.3	96.1	94.5	87.8	82.9	74.4
19.	Number of farms[18, 19]	. . .	. . .	. . .	. . .	. . .	. . .	143,807	179,889	195,953
20.	Acres in farms[18, 19]	. . .	. . .	. . .	. . .	. . .	. . .	17,997,493	20,472,141	21,712,420
21.	Acres improved land in farms[20]	. . .	. . .	. . .	. . .	. . .	. . .	9,851,493	12,625,394	14,469,133
22.	Cropland harvested, acres[18, 19]	. . .	. . .	. . .	. . .	. . .	. . .	NA	NA	NA
23.	Percentage increase in number of farms[18, 19]	. . .	. . .	. . .	. . .	. . .	. . .	. . .	25.1	8.9
24.	Percentage increase of land in farms[18, 19]	. . .	. . .	. . .	. . .	. . .	. . .	. . .	13.7	6.1
25.	Percentage increase of improved land in farms[20]	. . .	. . .	. . .	. . .	. . .	. . .	. . .	28.2	14.6

OHIO

1880	1890	1900	1910	1920	1930	1940	1950	1960	1970
3,198,062	3,672,329	4,157,545	4,767,121	5,759,394	6,646,697	6,907,612	7,946,627	9,706,397	10,652,017
20.0	14.8	13.2	14.7	20.8	15.4	3.9	15.0	22.1	9.7
532,802	474,267	485,216	609,576	992,273	887,303	260,915	1,039,015	1,759,770	945,620
6.4	5.8	5.5	5.2	5.4	5.4	5.2	5.3	5.4	5.2
78.5	90.1	102.1	117.0	141.4	161.6	168.0	193.8	236.6	260.0
21	21	21	22	22	24	23	23	24	23
3,117,920	3,584,805	4,060,204	4,654,897	5,571,893	6,335,173	6,566,531	7,428,222	8,909,698	9,646,997
19.8	15.0	13.3	14.6	19.7	13.7	3.7	13.1	20.0	8.3
79,900	87,113	96,901	111,452	186,187	309,304	339,461	513,072	786,097	970,477
26.4	9.0	11.2	15.0	66.5	66.1	9.7	51.1	53.2	23.5
2.5	2.4	2.3	2.3	3.2	4.7	4.9	6.5	8.1	9.1
. . .	. . .	. . .	. . .	. . .	. . .	. . .	. . .	. . .	. . .
1,030,769	1,510,153	1,998,382	2,665,143	3,677,136	4,507,371	4,612,986	5,346,336[c] / 5,578,274[d]	6,537,805[c] / 7,123,162[d]	8,025,775[d]
50.9	46.5	32.3	33.4	38.0	22.6	2.3	15.9[c]	22.3[c] / 27.7[d]	12.7[d]
2,167,293	2,162,176	2,159,163	2,101,978	2,082,258	2,139,326	2,294,626	2,600,291[c] / 2,368,353[d]	3,168,592[c] / 2,583,235[d]	2,626,242[d]
9.3	-0.2	-0.1	-2.6	-0.9	2.7	7.3	13.3[c]	21.9[c] / 9.1[d]	1.7[d]
32.2	41.1	48.1	55.9	63.8	67.8	66.8	67.3[c] / 70.2[d]	67.4[c] / 73.4[d]	75.3[d]
67.8	58.9	51.9	44.1	36.2	32.2	33.2	32.7[c] / 29.8[d]	32.6[c] / 26.6[d]	24.7[d]
247,189	251,430	276,719	272,045	256,695	219,296	233,783	199,359	140,353	111,332
24,529,226	23,352,408	24,501,985	24,105,708	23,515,888	21,514,059	21,907,523	20,969,411	18,506,796	17,111,459
18,081,091	18,338,824	19,244,472	19,227,969	18,542,353	. . .	. . .	. . .	. . .	. . .
9,086,811	10,038,131	11,614,165	11,431,610	11,783,788	10,115,652	9,771,609	10,295,590	9,743,467	8,515,275
26.1	1.7	10.1	-1.7	-5.6	-10.4	-8.4	-9.6	-20.7	-20.7
13.0	-4.8	4.9	-1.6	-2.4	-3.2	-4.2	-4.4	-7.4	-7.5
25.0	1.4	4.9	-0.1	-3.6	. . .	. . .	. . .	. . .	. . .

General Population, Agriculture, and Manufacturing Statistics, 1790-1970—OHIO (Cont.)

Item No.		1790 (or 1789)	1800	1810	1820	1830	1840	1850	1860	1870
26.	Average acreage per farm[18,19]	...	...	...	...	...	...	125.2	113.8	110.8
27.	Percentage increase in cropland harvested[18,19]	...	...	...	...	...	...	...	NA	NA
28.	Value of farms, dollars[18,19]	...	...	...	...	...	...	358,758,603	678,132,991	843,572,181
29.	Value of farms, percent increase[18,19]	...	...	...	...	...	...	...	89.0	24.4
30.	Average value per farm, dollars[18,19]	...	...	...	...	...	...	2,495	3,770	4,305
31.	Farms operated by owners[21,22,23,24,25,26,27]	...	...	...	...	...	...	...	...	...
32.	Value of livestock on farms, dollars[28,29,30,36]	...	...	...	...	...	...	44,121,741	80,384,819	96,240,422[b]
33.	Average value of livestock per farm, dollars[19,28,29,30,36]	...	...	...	...	...	...	307	447	491[b]
34.	Production of wheat in bushels[31,32,35,36]	...	...	...	...	...	16,571,661	14,487,351	15,119,047	27,882,159
35.	Percent of total production of wheat[31,32,33,35,36]	...	...	...	...	...	20.0	14.4	8.7	9.7
36.	Production of corn in bushels[36,37,38,39]	...	...	...	...	...	...	59,078,695	73,543,190	67,501,144
37.	Percent of total production of corn[36,37,38,39]	...	...	...	...	...	...	10.0	8.8	8.9
38.	Production of oats in bushels[31,35,36]	...	...	...	...	...	14,393,103	13,472,742	15,409,234	25,347,549
39.	Percent of total production of oats[31,35,36]	...	...	...	...	...	11.7	9.2	8.9	9.0
40.	Production of soybeans in bushels[36,40,41]	...	...	...	...	...	...	...	...	...
41.	Percent of total production of soybeans[34,36,40,41]	...	...	...	...	...	...	...	...	...
42.	Production of hay crops in tons[31,34,42,43,44]	...	...	...	...	...	1,022,037	1,443,142	1,564,502	2,289,565
43.	Percent of total production of hay crops[31,34,42,43,44]	...	...	...	...	...	10.0	10.4	8.2	8.4
44.	Number of manufacturing establishments[44,46,47,48]	...	...	...	...	...	...	10,622	11,123	22,773
45.	Capital of manufacturing establishments[45,46,47,48]	...	...	...	...	...	...	29,019,538	57,295,303	141,923,964
46.	Average number of wage earners[45,46,47,48]	...	...	...	...	...	...	51,491	75,602	137,202
47.	Total wages[45,46,47,48]	...	...	...	...	...	...	13,467,156	22,302,989	49,066,488
48.	Cost of materials used in manufacturing[45,46,47,48]	...	...	...	...	...	...	34,678,019	69,800,270	157,131,697
49.	Value of manufactured product[45,46,47,48]	...	...	...	...	...	...	62,692,279	121,691,148	269,713,610

b. Values in gold

c. Previous urban definition

d. Present urban definition

General Population, Agriculture, and Manufacturing Statistics, 1790-1970

OHIO

1880	1890	1900	1910	1920	1930	1940	1950	1960	1970
99.2	92.9	88.5	88.6	91.6	98.1	93.7	105.2	131.9	153.7
NA	10.5	15.7	-1.6	3.1	-5.5	-5.9	-5.0	-5.8	-12.6
1,127,497,353	1,050,031,828	1,036,615,180	1,654,152,406	2,661,435,949	1,693,030,716	1,443,917,176	2,858,969,000	4,573,139,000	6,819,215,000
33.7	-6.9	-1.3	59.6	60.9	-13.0	13.0	53.0	23.4	49.1
4,561	4,176	3,746	6,080	10,368	7,720	6,176	14,341	32,583	61,251
199,562	193,895	200,788	192,104	177,986	159,849	171,156	162,995	117,039	98,032
103,707,730	116,181,690	125,954,616	197,332,112	286,776,386	216,139,273	156,908,404	352,494,542	426,117,231	405,840,000
420	462	455	725	1,121	986	671	1,768	3,036	3,645
46,014,869	35,559,208	50,376,800	30,663,704	58,124,351	30,289,579	37,074,406	46,596,000	29,499,714	35,927,000
10.0	7.6	7.6	4.5	6.1	3 8	5.2	4.6	2.8	2.6
111,877,124	113,892,318	152,055,390	157,513,300	149,844,626	102,177,194	156,303,520	168,046,185	246,708,000	232,078,000
6.4	5.4	5.7	6.2	6.4	4.8	6.8	6.0	5.8	5.7
28,664,505	40,136,732	42,050,910	57,591,046	46,818,330	44,730,590	30,764,247	42,281,470	47,930,525	29,870,000
7.0	5.0	4.5	5.7	4.4	4.5	3.5	3.7	4.8	3.3
. . .	. . .	. . .	. . .	. . .	316,462	10,293,393	18,794,324	35,430,327	68,799,000
. . .	. . .	. . .	. . .	. . .		3.6	11.8	8.8	6.9	6.1
2,212,133	3,981,070	3,506,654	4,076,609	3,716,036	3,456,552	3,280,279	3,003,753	3,564,094	2,913,000
6.3	6.0	4.9	4.6	4.1	4.1	4.0	3.4	3.3	2.3
20,699	28,673	32,398	15,138	16,125	11,855	10,070			
188,939,614	402,793,019	605,792,266	1,300,733,000	3,748,744,000	. . .	. . .			
183,609	292,982	345,869	446,934	730,733	741,143	598,397			
62,103,800	128,447,799	153,955,330	245,450,000	944,652,000	1,102,166,000	812,676,000			
215,334,258	341,016,464	447,849,677	824,202,000	2,911,948,000	3,138,099,000	2,459,192,000			
348,298,390	641,688,064	832,438,113	1,437,936,000	5,100,309,000	6,027,903,000	4,584,666,000			

See following tables

SOUTH DAKOTA

Item No.		1790 (or 1789)	1800	1810	1820	1830	1840	1850	1860	1870
1.	Population[1]	...	...	...	...	...	...	...	4,837[a]	11,776
2.	Decennial rates of increase in population over preceding census[2]	...	... [a]	...	...	...	...	...	...	193.2[a]
3.	Increase in population over previous census[1, 3]	...	...	...	...	...	...	...	4,837[a]	9,344
4.	Percent distribution of population[4]	...	...	...	...	...	...	...	...	...
5.	Population per square mile of land area[5, 6]	...	...	...	...	...	...	...	...	...
6.	Membership of House of Representatives at each apportionment[7]	...	...	...	...	...	...	...	...	...
7.	White population[8, 9, 10]	...	...	...	...	...	...	...	2,576[a]	12,887[a]
8.	Percent increase in white population over preceding census[9, 10, 11]	...	...	...	...	...	...	...	...	400.3[a]
9.	Negro population[8, 9, 10]	...	...	...	...	...	...	...	...	94[a]
10.	Percentage increase in Negro population over preceding census[9, 10, 11, 12, 13, 14]	...	...	...	...	...	...	...	...	...
11.	Percent Negro in total population[1, 8, 9, 10, 14, 15]	...	...	...	...	...	...	...	...	0.7
12.	Number of slaves in the area enumerated in 1790 and in the added area[16]	...	...	...	...	...	...	...	...	...
13.	Urban population[17]	...	...	...	...	...	...	...	...	...
14.	Percent urban increase[17]	...	...	...	...	...	...	...	...	...
15.	Rural population[17]	...	...	...	...	...	...	...	...	11,776
16.	Percent rural increase over preceding census[17]	...	...	...	...	...	...	...	...	...
17.	Percent of urban to total population[17]	...	...	...	...	...	...	...	...	...
18.	Percent of rural to total population[17]	...	...	...	...	...	...	...	...	100.0
19.	Number of farms[18, 19]	...	...	...	...	...	...	...	...	...
20.	Acres in farms[18, 19]	...	...	...	...	...	...	...	...	...
21.	Acres improved land in farms[20]	...	...	...	...	...	...	...	...	...
22.	Cropland harvested, acres[18, 19]	...	...	...	...	...	...	...	...	...
23.	Percentage increase in number of farms[18, 19]	...	...	...	...	...	...	...	...	...
24.	Percentage increase of land in farms[18, 19]	...	...	...	...	...	...	...	...	...
25.	Percentage increase of improved land in farms[20]	...	...	...	...	...	...	...	...	...

General Population, Agriculture, and Manufacturing Statistics, 1790-1970

SOUTH DAKOTA

1880	1890	1900	1910	1920	1930	1940	1950	1960	1970
98,268	348,600	401,570	583,888	636,547	692,849	642,961	652,740	680,514	665,507
734.5	254.7	15.2	45.4	9.0	8.8	-7.2	1.5	4.3	-2.2
120,996	376,350	55,079	182,318	52,659	56,302	-49,888	9,779	27,774	-15,007
0.2	0.6	0.5	0.6	0.6	0.6	0.5	0.4	0.4	0.3
...	4.5	5.2	7.6	8.3	9.0	8.4	8.5	9.0	8.8
2	2	2	3	3	2	2	2	2	2
96,955	328,010	380,714	563,771	619,147	670,269	619,075	628,504	653,098	630,333
933.2	283.3	16.1	4.8	9.8	8.2	-7.6	1.5	3.9	-3.5
288	541	465	817	832	646	474	727	1,114	1,627
326.6	127.9	14.0	75.7	1.8	-22.4	-26.6	53.4	53.2	46.1
0.3	0.2	0.1	0.1	0.1	0.1	0.1	1.1	1.6	0.2
...	...	...	...	...	...	...	216,157c / 216,710d	265,328c / 267,180d	...
7,208	28,555	40,936	76,469	101,872	130,907	158,087			296,628d
...	296.2	43.4	86.8	33.2	28.5	20.8	36.7c / 23.3d	22.7c / 23.3d	11.0d
91,060	320,045	360,634	507,419	534,675	561,942	484,874	436,583c / 436,030d	415,186c / 413,334d	368,879d
673.3	251.5	12.7	40.7	5.4	5.1	-13.7	-10.0c / -5.2d	-4.9c / -5.2d	-10.8d
7.3	8.2	10.2	13.1	16.0	18.9	24.6	33.1c / 33.2d	39.0c / 39.3d	44.6d
92.7	91.8	89.8	86.9	84.0	81.1	75.4	66.9c / 66.8d	61.0c / 60.7d	55.4d
13,645	50,158	52,622	77,644	74,637	83,157	72,454	66,452	55,727	45,726
2,772,811	11,396,460	19,070,616	26,016,892	34,636,491	36,470,083	39,473,584	44,785,529	44,850,666	45,584,164
890,870	5,959,293	11,285,983	15,827,208	18,199,250	...	...	...	...	...
NA	5,647,880	8,843,905	12,226,772	14,655,116	17,856,178	12,297,291	17,527,893	14,236,384	12,634,488
...	267.6	4.9	47.6	-3.9	11.4	-12.9	-8.3	-16.1	-17.9
...	311.0	67.3	36.4	33.1	5.3	8.2	13.5	0.1	1.6
...	681.2	62.2	40.2	15.0	...	...	...	...	...

General Population, Agriculture, and Manufacturing Statistics, 1790-1970—SOUTH DAKOTA (Cont.)

Item No.	1790 (or 1789)	1800	1810	1820	1830	1840	1850	1860	1870
26. Average acreage per farm[18, 19]	...	...	...	...	...	...	...	...	...
27. Percentage increase in cropland harvested[18, 19]	...	...	...	...	...	...	...	...	...
28. Value of farms, dollars[18, 19]	...	...	...	...	...	...	...	...	...
29. Value of farms, percent increase[18, 19]	...	...	...	...	...	...	...	...	...
30. Average value per farm, dollars[18, 19]	...	...	...	...	...	...	...	...	...
31. Farms operated by owners[21, 22, 23, 24, 25, 26, 27]	...	...	...	...	...	...	...	...	...
32. Value of livestock on farms, dollars[28, 29, 30, 36]	...	...	...	...	...	...	...	...	...
33. Average value of livestock per farm, dollars[19, 28, 29, 30, 36]	...	...	...	...	...	...	...	...	...
34. Production of wheat in bushels[31, 32, 35, 36]	...	...	...	...	...	...	...	945[a]	170,662[a]
35. Percent of total production of wheat[31, 32, 33, 35, 36]	...	...	...	...	...	...	...	...	...
36. Production of corn in bushels[36, 37, 38, 39]	...	...	...	...	...	...	...	...	...
37. Percent of total production of corn[36, 37, 38, 39]	...	...	...	...	...	...	...	...	...
38. Production of oats in bushels[31, 35, 36]	...	...	...	...	...	...	...	2,540[a]	114,327[a]
39. Percent of total production of oats[31, 35, 36]	...	...	...	...	...	...	...	...	...
40. Production of soybeans in bushels[36, 40, 41]	...	...	...	...	...	...	...	...	...
41. Percent of total production of soybeans[34, 36, 40, 41]	...	...	...	...	...	...	...	...	...
42. Production of hay crops in tons[31, 34, 42, 43, 44]	...	...	...	...	...	...	...	855[a]	13,347[a]
43. Percent of total production of hay crops[31, 34, 42, 43, 44]	...	...	...	...	...	...	...	b	b
44. Number of manufacturing establishments[45, 46, 47, 48]	...	...	...	...	...	...	...	...	17[a]
45. Capital of manufacturing establishments[45, 46, 47, 48]	...	...	...	...	...	...	...	...	79,200[a]
46. Average number of wage earners[45, 46, 47, 48]	...	...	...	...	...	...	...	...	91[a]
47. Total wages[45, 46, 47, 48]	...	...	...	...	...	...	...	...	21,106[a]
48. Cost of materials used in manufacturing[45, 46, 47, 48]	...	...	...	...	...	...	...	...	105,997[a]
49. Value of manufactured product[45, 46, 47, 48]	...	...	...	...	...	...	...	...	178,570[a]

a. Dakota Territory (see e)

b. Less than 0.1%

c. Previous urban definition

d. Present urban definition

e. North Dakota and South Dakota admitted as States in 1889. Figures for 1879 obtained by consolidating data for the counties which then occupied the areas now known as North Dakota and South Dakota, respectively. The 1869 and 1859 figures are for Dakota Territory.

f. Probable census error

44

General Population, Agriculture, and Manufacturing Statistics, 1790-1970

SOUTH DAKOTA

1880	1890	1900	1910	1920	1930	1940	1950	1960	1970
203.2	227.2	362.4	335.1	464.1	438.6	544.8	674.0	804.8	996.9
NA	NA	56.6	38.3	19.9	13.1	8.2	42.5	−18.8	−11.3
13,825,970	107,466,335	220,133,190	1,005,080,807	2,472,893,681	1,285,153,538	505,452,178	1,401,787,000	2,276,544,000	3,814,776,000
. . .	677.3	104.8	356.6	146.0	−48.0	−60.7	177.3	62.4	67.6
1,013	2,143	4,183	12,945	33,132	15,455	6,976	21,095	40,852	83,427
. . .	43,555	41,171	57,984	47,815	45,609	33,803	46,031	40,783	37,849
. . .	29,689,509	65,173,432	127,229,200	238,128,771	186,622,264	104,156,465	364,750,026	549,434,105	837,900,000
. . .	592	1,238	1,639	3,196	2,244	1,437	5,489	9,859	18,324
1,092,946[e]	16,541,138	41,889,380	47,059,590	31,086,995	34,044,975	17,592,727	33,488,000	17,240,094	39,282,000
2.4[e]	3.5	6.4	6.9	3.3	4.3	2.5	3.3	1.6	2.9
. . .	13,152,008	32,402,540	55,558,737	69,060,782	84,569,812	40,755,611	76,149,324	79,774,000	102,336,000
. . .	0.6	1.2	2.2	2.9	4.0	1.8	2.7	1.9	2.5
1,488,321[e]	7,469,846	19,412,490	43,565,676	51,091,904	62,480,531	43,101,900	62,578,547	39,751,143	102,336,000
. . .	0.9	2.1	4.3	4.8	6.3	5.0	5.5	4.0	11.3
. . .	. . .	. . .	. . .	. . .	419	5,369	386,845	1,510,924	4,323,000
. . .	. . .	. . .	. . .	. . .	. . .	. . .[b]	0.2	0.3	0.4
276,484[e]	1,541,524	2,332,464	3,573,286	3,917,259	2,645,277	1,727,320	2,966,293	3,263,593	5,519,000
0.8[e]	2.3	3.3	4.1	4.3	3.1	2.1	3.3	3.1	4.3
251[a]	499	1,639	1,020	1,414	615	468			
771,428	3,207,796	7,578,895	13,018,000	30,933,000	. . .	. . .			
868	2,011	3,121	3,602	6,382	6,535	5,538			
339,375	832,693	1,544,409	2,297,000	7,905,000	8,132,000	6,036,000			
1,523,761	3,523,840	7,827,110	11,476,000	42,986,000	75,016,000	61,217,000			
2,373,970	5,682,748	12,231,239	17,870,000	62,171,000	97,698,000	81,172,000			

WISCONSIN

Item No.		1790 (or 1789)	1800	1810	1820	1830	1840	1850	1860	1870
1.	Population[1]	. . .	. . .	. . .	. . .	. . .	30,945[a]	305,391	775,881	1,054,670
2.	Decennial rates of increase in population over preceding census[2]	. . .	. . .	. . .	. . .	. . .	. . .	886.9	154.1	35.9
3.	Increase in population over previous census[1, 3]	. . .	. . .	. . .	. . .	. . .	30,945	274,446	470,490	278,789
4.	Percent distribution of population[4]	. . .	. . .	. . .	. . .	. . .	0.2	1.3	2.5	2.7
5.	Population per square mile of land area[5, 6]	. . .	. . .	. . .	. . .	. . .	. . .	5.5	14.0	19.1
6.	Membership of House of Representatives at each apportionment[7]	. . .	. . .	. . .	. . .	. . .	2	3	6	8
7.	White population[8, 9, 10]	. . .	. . .	. . .	. . .	. . .	30,749	304,756	773,693	1,051,351
8.	Percent increase in white population over preceding census[9, 10, 11]	. . .	. . .	. . .	. . .	. . .	. . .	891.1	153.9	35.9
9.	Negro population[8, 9, 10]	. . .	. . .	. . .	. . .	. . .	196	635	1,171	2,113
10.	Percentage increase in Negro population over preceding census[9, 10, 11, 12, 13, 14]	. . .	. . .	. . .	. . .	. . .	. . .	224.0	84.4	80.4
11.	Percent Negro in total population[1, 8, 9, 10, 14, 15]	. . .	. . .	. . .	. . .	. . .	. . .	0.2	0.2	0.2
12.	Number of slaves in the area enumerated in 1790 and in the added area[16]	. . .	. . .	. . .	. . .	31	11	. . .	. . .	. . .
13.	Urban population[17]	. . .	. . .	. . .	. . .	. . .	. . .	28,623	111,874	207,099
14.	Percent urban increase[17]	. . .	. . .	. . .	. . .	. . .	. . .	. . .	290.9	85.1
15.	Rural population[17]	. . .	. . .	. . .	. . .	. . .	30,945	276,768	664,007	847,571
16.	Percent rural increase over preceding census[17]	. . .	. . .	. . .	. . .	. . .	. . .	794.4	139.9	27.6
17.	Percent of urban to total population[17]	. . .	. . .	. . .	. . .	. . .	. . .	9.4	14.4	19.6
18.	Percent of rural to total population[17]	. . .	. . .	. . .	. . .	. . .	100.0	90.6	85.6	80.4
19.	Number of farms[18, 19]	. . .	. . .	. . .	. . .	. . .	. . .	20,177	69,270	102,904
20.	Acres in farms[18, 19]	. . .	. . .	. . .	. . .	. . .	. . .	2,976,658	7,893,587	11,715,321
21.	Acres improved land in farms[20]	. . .	. . .	. . .	. . .	. . .	. . .	1,045,499	3,746,167	5,899,343
22.	Cropland harvested, acres[18, 19]	. . .	. . .	. . .	. . .	. . .	. . .	NA	NA	NA
23.	Percentage increase in number of farms[18, 19]	. . .	. . .	. . .	. . .	. . .	. . .	. . .	243.3	48.6
24.	Percentage increase of land in farms[18, 19]	. . .	. . .	. . .	. . .	. . .	. . .	. . .	165.2	48.4
25.	Percentage increase of improved land in farms[20]	. . .	. . .	. . .	. . .	. . .	. . .	. . .	258.3	57 .5

WISCONSIN

1880	1890	1900	1910	1920	1930	1940	1950	1960	1970
1,315,497	1,693,330	2,069,042	2,333,860	2,632,067	2,939,006	3,137,587	3,434,575	3,951,777	4,417,731
24.7	28.7	22.2	12.8	12.8	11.7	6.8	9.5	15.1	11.8
260,827	371,383	376,036	264,818	298,207	306,939	198,581	296,988	517,202	465,954
2.6	2.7	2.7	2.5	2.5	2.4	2.4	2.3	2.2	2.2
23.8	30.6	37.4	42.2	47.6	53.7	57.3	62.8	72.6	81.1
9	10	11	11	11	10	10	10	10	9
1,309,618	1,680,828	2,057,911	2,320,555	2,616,938	2,916,255	3,112,752	3,392,690	3,858,903	4,258,959
24.6	28.3	22.4	12.8	11.3	11.4	6.7	9.0	13.7	10.4
2,702	2,444	2,542	2,900	5,201	10,739	12,158	28,182	74,546	128,224
27.9	9.5	4.0	14.1	79.3	106.5	13.2	131.8	164.5	72.0
0.2	0.1	0.1	0.1	0.2	0.4	0.4	0.8	1.9	2.9
. . .	. . .	. . .	. . .	. . .	. . .	. . .	. . .	. . .	. . .
317,204	562,286	790,213	1,004,320	1,244,858	1,553,843	1,679,144	1,949,260[c] / 1,987,888[d]	2,452,295[c] / 2,522,179[d]	2,910,418[d]
53.2	77.3	40.5	27.1	24.0	24.8	8.1	16.1[c]	25.8[c] / 26.9[d]	15.4[d]
998,293	1,131,044	1,278,829	1,329,540	1,387,209	1,385,163	1,458,443	1,485,315[c] / 1,446,687[d]	1,499,482[c] / 1,429,598[d]	1,507,313[d]
17.8	13.3	13.1	4.0	4.3	−0.1	5.3	1.8[c]	1.0[c] / −1.2[d]	5.4[d]
24.1	33.2	38.2	43.0	47.3	52.9	53.5	56.8[c] / 57.9[d]	62.1[c] / 63.8[d]	65.9[d]
75.9	66.8	61.8	57.0	52.7	47.1	46.5	43.2[c] / 42.1[d]	37.9[c] / 36.2[d]	34.1[d]
134,322	146,409	169,795	177,127	189,295	181,767	186,735	168,561	131,215	98,973
15,353,118	16,787,988	19,862,727	21,060,066	22,148,223	21,874,155	22,876,494	23,221,095	21,156,223	18,109,273
9,162,528	9,793,931	11,246,972	11,907,606	12,452,216					
5,825,463	6,738,193	8,214,711	8,555,080	9,590,633	9,618,331	9,815,964	10,112,027	9,599,094	8,133,848
30.5	9.0	16.0	4.3	6.9	−4.0	2.7	−9.7	−22.1	−24.6
31.1	9.3	18.3	6.0	5.2	−1.2	4.6	−1.5	−8.9	−14.4
55.3	6.9	14.8	5.9	4.6	. . .	. . .	. . .	. . .	. . .

General Population, Agriculture, and Manufacturing Statistics, 1790-1970—WISCONSIN (Cont.)

Item No.	1790 (or 1789)	1800	1810	1820	1830	1840	1850	1860	1870
26. Average acreage per farm[18, 19]	. . .	. . .	. . .	. . .	. . .	. . .	147.5	114.0	113.8
27. Percentage increase in cropland harvested[18, 19]	. . .	. . .	. . .	. . .	. . .	. . .	NA	NA	NA
28. Value of farms, dollars[18, 19]	. . .	. . .	. . .	. . .	. . .	. . .	28,528,563	131,117,164	240,331,251
29. Value of farms, percent increase[18, 19]	. . .	. . .	. . .	. . .	. . .	. . .	. . .	359.6	83.3
30. Average value per farm, dollars[18, 19]	. . .	. . .	. . .	. . .	. . .	. . .	1,414	1,893	2,335
31. Farms operated by owners[21, 22, 23, 24, 25, 26, 27]	. . .	. . .	. . .	. . .	. . .	. . .	. . .	. . .	. . .
32. Value of livestock on farms, dollars[28, 29, 30, 36]	. . .	. . .	. . .	. . .	. . .	. . .	4,897,385	17,807,375	36,248,706[b]
33. Average value of livestock per farm, dollars[19, 28, 29, 30, 36]	. . .	. . .	. . .	. . .	. . .	. . .	243	257	352[b]
34. Production of wheat in bushels[31, 32, 35, 36]	. . .	. . .	. . .	. . .	. . .	212,116	4,286,131	15,657,458	25,606,344
35. Percent of total production of wheat[31, 32, 33, 35, 36]	. . .	. . .	. . .	. . .	. . .	0.2	4.3	9.1	8.9
36. Production of corn in bushels[36, 37, 38, 39]	. . .	. . .	. . .	. . .	. . .	. . .	1,988,979	7,517,300	15,033,998
37. Percent of total production of corn[36, 37, 38, 39]	. . .	. . .	. . .	. . .	. . .	. . .	0.3	0.9	2.0
38. Production of oats in bushels[31, 35, 36]	. . .	. . .	. . .	. . .	. . .	406,514	3,414,672	11,059,260	20,180,016
39. Percent of total production of oats[31, 35, 36]	. . .	. . .	. . .	. . .	. . .	. . .	2.3	6.4	7.2
40. Production of soybeans in bushels[36, 40, 41]	. . .	. . .	. . .	. . .	. . .	. . .	. . .	. . .	. . .
41. Percent of total production of soybeans[36, 40, 41]	. . .	. . .	. . .	. . .	. . .	. . .	. . .	. . .	. . .
42. Production of hay crops in tons[31, 34, 42, 43, 44]	. . .	. . .	. . .	. . .	. . .	30,938	275,662	855,037	1,287,651
43. Percent of total production of hay crops[31, 34, 42, 43, 44]	. . .	. . .	. . .	. . .	. . .	. . .	2.0	4.5	4.7
44. Number of manufacturing establishments[46, 47, 48]	. . .	. . .	. . .	. . .	. . .	. . .	1,262	3,064	7,013
45. Capital of manufacturing establishments[45, 46, 47, 48]	. . .	. . .	. . .	. . .	. . .	. . .	3,382,148	15,831,581	41,981,872
46. Average number of wage earners[45, 46, 47, 48]	. . .	. . .	. . .	. . .	. . .	. . .	6,089	15,414	43,910
47. Total wages[45, 46, 47, 48]	. . .	. . .	. . .	. . .	. . .	. . .	1,712,496	4,268,708	13,575,642
48. Cost of materials used in manufacturing[45, 46, 47, 48]	. . .	. . .	. . .	. . .	. . .	. . .	5,414,931	17,137,334	45,851,266
49. Value of manufactured product[45, 46, 47, 48]	. . .	. . .	. . .	. . .	. . .	. . .	9,293,068	27,849,467	77,214,326

a. Includes population of that part of Minnesota northeast of the Mississippi River.

b. Values in gold

c. Previous urban definition

d. Present urban definition

48

1880	1890	1900	1910	1920	1930	1940	1950	1960	1970
114.3	114.7	117.0	118.9	117.0	120.3	122.5	137.8	161.2	183.0
NA	15.7	21.9	4.1	12.1	2.8	2.1	3.0	-5.1	-15.3
357,709,507	447,524,507	686,147,660	1,201,632,723	2,187,881,973	1,731,517,017	1,188,559,407	2,056,925,000	2,796,049,000	4,201,294,000
48.8	33.5	43.7	75.1	82.1	-20.9	-31.4	73.1	35.9	50.3
2,663	3,262	4,041	6,784	11,558	9,526	6,365	12,203	21,309	42,448
122,163	129,681	146,799	151,022	159,610	146,987	142,728	141,652	115,524	91,978
46,508,643	63,784,377	96,327,649	158,529,483	321,350,250	307,384,493	256,503,605	647,940,946	781,784,850	998,620
346	436	567	895	1,703	1,691	1,374	3,844	5,958	10,090
24,884,689	11,698,922	9,005,170	2,641,476	7,328,444	1,835,704	969,713	2,084,000	1,816,643	1,422,000
5.4	2.5	1.4	0.4	0.8	0.2	0.1	0.2	0.2	0.1
34,230,579	34,024,216	53,309,810	49,163,034	44,547,398	26,019,264	44,552,990	83,974,114	184,990,000	143,520,000
2.0	1.6	2.0	1.9	1.9	1.2	1.9	3.0	4.3	3.5
32,905,320	60,739,052	84,040,800	71,349,038	68,296,223	68,694,665	64,514,885	112,840,761	121,399,193	104,594,000
8.1	7.5	8.9	7.1	6.5	6.9	7.4	9.9	12.1	11.5
...	...	...	...	...	18,451	166,355	273,702	1,851,320	3,213,000
...	...	...	...	...	...	0.2	0.1	0.4	0.3
1,907,429	2,981,521	3,066,324	4,423,385	5,043,708	6,226,633	5,764,323	5,705,604	8,866,854	10,601,000
5.4	4.5	4.3	5.1	5.6	7.3	7.0	6.4	8.3	8.3
7,674	10,417	16,187	9,721	10,393	7,431	6,717			
73,821,802	246,515,404	330,568,779	605,657,000	1,361,729,000	...	...			
57,109	120,006	142,076	182,583	263,949	264,745	200,897			
18,814,917	42,958,267	58,407,597	93,905,000	290,441,000	352,491,000	251,947,000		See following tables	
85,796,178	145,437,016	208,838,167	346,356,000	1,127,275,000	1,206,840,000	917,902,000			
128,255,480	248,546,164	360,818,942	590,305,000	1,846,984,000	2,156,682,000	1,604,507,000			

THE MIDWEST
REGIONAL TOTALS

Item No.		1790 (or 1789)	1800	1810	1820	1830	1840	1850	1860	1870
1.	Population[1]	. . .	51,006	292,107	859,305	1,610,473	3,351,542	5,403,595	9,096,716	12,981,111
2.	Decennial rates of increase in population over preceding census[2]	. . .	. . .	472.7	194.2	87.4	108.1	61.2	68.3	42.7
3.	Increase in population over previous census[1, 3]	. . .	. . .	241,101	567,198	751,168	1,741,069	2,052,053	3,693,121	3,884,395
4.	Percent distribution of population[4]	. . .	1.0	4.1	8.9	12.5	19.6	23.3	28.9	33.7
5.	Population per square mile of land area[1, 5, 6]	. . .	0.07	0.4	1.14	2.1	4.5	7.2	12.1	17.3
6.	Membership of House of Representatives at each apportionment[7]	. . .	1	8	19	32	50	59	75	98
7.	White population[8, 9, 10]	. . .	. . .	286,097	841,045	1,568,930	3,262,195	5,267,988	8,899,969	12,698,503
8.	Percent increase in white population over preceding census[8, 9, 10, 11]	. . .	. . .	433.8	192.0	86.5	107.9	61.5	68.9	42.7
9.	Negro population[8, 9, 10]	. . .	. . .	7,072	18,260	41,543	89,347	135,607	184,239	273,080
10.	Percentage increase in Negro population over preceding census[9, 10, 11, 12, 13, 14]	. . .	. . .	1,013.7	158.2	127.5	115.1	51.8	35.9	48.2
11.	Percent Negro in total population[1, 8, 9, 10, 14, 15]	. . .	. . .	2.4	2.1	2.6	2.7	2.5	2.0	2.1
12.	Number of slaves in the area enumerated in 1790 and in the added area[16]	. . .	135	3,304	11,329	25,879	58,604	87,422	114,948	. . .
13.	Urban population[17]	. . .	. . .	2,540	9,642	41,635	129,385	499,413	1,263,242	2,702,367
14.	Percent urban increase[17]	. . .	. . .	. . .	279.6	331.8	210.8	286.0	152.9	113.9
15.	Rural population[17]	. . .	51,006	289,567	849,663	1,568,838	3,222,157	4,904,182	7,833,474	10,278,744
16.	Percent rural increase over preceding census[17]	. . .	. . .	467.7	193.4	84.6	105.4	52.2	59.7	31.2
17.	Percent of urban to total population[17]	. . .	. . .	0.9	1.1	2.6	3.9	9.2	13.9	20.8
18.	Percent of rural to total population[17]	. . .	100.0	99.1	98.9	97.4	96.1	90.8	86.1	79.2
19.	Number of farms[18, 19, 49]	. . .	. . .	. . .	. . .	. . .	. . .	437,597	772,165	1,125,078
20.	Acres in farms[18, 19, 49]	. . .	. . .	. . .	. . .	. . .	. . .	62,686,490	107,899,590	139,215,269
21.	Acres improved land in farms[20, 50]	. . .	. . .	. . .	. . .	. . .	. . .	26,680,332	52,308,699	78,409,509
22.	Cropland harvested, acres[18, 19]	. . .	. . .	. . .	. . .	. . .	. . .			
23.	Percentage increase in number of farms[18, 19, 49]	. . .	. . .	. . .	. . .	. . .	. . .	. . .	76.5	45.7
24.	Percentage increase of land in farms[18, 19, 49]	. . .	. . .	. . .	. . .	. . .	. . .	. . .	72.1	29.0
25.	Percentage increase of improved land in farms[20, 50]	. . .	. . .	. . .	. . .	. . .	. . .	. . .	96.1	49.8

General Population, Agriculture, and Manufacturing Statistics, 1790-1970

THE MIDWEST
REGIONAL TOTALS

1880	1890	1900	1910	1920	1930	1940	1950	1960	1970
17,364,111	22,410,417	26,333,004	29,888,542	34,019,792	38,594,100	40,143,332	44,460,762	51,619,139	56,571,663
33.8	29.1	17.5	13.5	13.8	13.4	4.0	10.8	16.1	9.6
4,383,000	5,046,306	3,922,587	3,555,538	4,131,250	4,574,308	1,549,232	4,317,430	7,158,377	4,952,524
34.6	35.6	34.6	32.4	32.1	31.3	30.4	29.4	28.8	27.8
23.1	29.8	35.0	39.7	45.2	51.3	53.4	59.1	68.6	75.2
117	128	136	143	143	137	131	129	125	121
16,961,423	21,913,813	25,775,870	29,279,243	33,164,249	37,249,272	38,639,970	42,119,384	48,002,617	51,641,183
33.6	29.2	17.6	13.6	13.3	12.3	3.7	9.0	14.0	7.6
385,621	431,112	495,751	543,498	793,075	1,262,234	1,420,318	2,227,876	3,446,037	4,571,550
41.2	11.8	15.0	9.6	45.9	59.2	12.5	56.9	54.7	32.7
2.2	1.9	1.9	1.8	2.3	3.3	3.5	5.0	6.7	8.1
. . .	. . .	. . .	. . .	. . .	. . .	. . .	. . .	. . .	. . .
4,198,442	7,418,101	10,165,312	13,487,199	17,775,966	22,351,089	23,437,483	27,183,902[c] 28,490,932[d]	32,993,873[c] 35,481,254[d]	40,480,760[d]
55.4	76.7	37.0	32.7	31.8	25.7	4.9	16.0[c]	21.4[c] 24.5[d]	14.1[d]
13,165,669	14,992,316	16,167,692	16,401,343	16,243,826	16,243,011	16,705,849	17,276,860[c] 15,969,830[d]	18,625,266[c] 16,137,885[d]	16,090,903[d]
28.1	13.9	7.8	1.4	-1.0	–	2.8	3.4[c]	7.8[c] 1.1[d]	-0.3[d]
24.2	33.1	38.6	45.1	52.8	57.9	58.4	61.1[c] 64.1[d]	63.9[c] 68.7[d]	71.6[d]
75.8	66.9	61.4	54.9	47.7	42.1	41.6	38.9[c] 35.9[d]	36.1[c] 31.3[d]	28.4[d]
1,697,968	1,923,822	2,196,567	2,221,829	2,181,695	2,079,257	2,096,669	1,868,139	1,460,707	1,151,884
206,982,157	256,586,994	317,349,474	350,577,269	374,708,408	376,379,086	388,077,931	396,426,382	385,393,067	373,368,946
136,842,319	184,292,126	222,314,099	253,232,090	259,289,274	. . .	. . .	. . .	. . .	. . .
50.9	13.3	14.2	1.2	-1.8	-4.7	0.8	-10.8	-21.8	-21.1
48.6	24.0	24.0	10.5	6.9	4.5	3.1	2.2	-2.8	-3.1
74.5	34.7	20.6	13.9	2.4	. . .	. . .	. . .	. . .	. . .

General Population, Agriculture, and Manufacturing Statistics, 1790-1970—THE MIDWEST (Cont.)

Item No.		1790 (or 1789)	1800	1810	1820	1830	1840	1850	1860	1870
26.	Average acreage per farm[18, 19, 20, 50]	. . .	. . .	. . .	. . .	. . .	. . .	143.3	139.7	123.7
27.	Percentage increase in cropland harvested[18, 19]	. . .	. . .	. . .	. . .	. . .	. . .			
28.	Value of farms, dollars[18, 19, 49]	. . .	. . .	. . .	. . .	. . .	. . .	751,723,133	2,130,013,463	3,451,602,260
29.	Value of farms, percent increase[18, 19, 49]	. . .	. . .	. . .	. . .	. . .	. . .	. . .	183.0	62.0
30.	Average value per farm, dollars[18, 19, 49]	. . .	. . .	. . .	. . .	. . .	. . .	1,718	2,758	3,067
31.	Farms operated by owners[21, 22, 23, 24, 25, 26, 27]	. . .	. . .	. . .	. . .	. . .	. . .	. . .	. . .	. . .
32.	Value of livestock on farms, dollars[28, 29, 30, 36]	. . .	. . .	. . .	. . .	. . .	. . .	127,385,387	320,576,873	533,480,262[b]
33.	Average value of livestock per farm, dollars[19, 28, 29, 30, 36, 49]	. . .	. . .	. . .	. . .	. . .	. . .	291	415	474[b]
34.	Production of wheat in bushels[31, 32, 33, 35, 36]	. . .	. . .	. . .	. . .	. . .	27,517,732	43,842,038	95,005,130	104,934,540
35.	Percent of total production of wheat[31, 32, 33, 35, 36]	. . .	. . .	. . .	. . .	. . .	32.4	43.6	54.9	67.8
36.	Production of corn in bushels[36, 37, 38, 39]	. . .	. . .	. . .	. . .	. . .	. . .	222,208,502	406,166,733	439,244,945
37.	Percent of total production of corn[36, 37, 38, 39]	. . .	. . .	. . .	. . .	. . .	. . .	37.5	48.4	57.7
38.	Production of oats in bushels[31, 35, 36]	. . .	. . .	. . .	. . .	. . .	30,334,613	42,328,731	62,953,218	159,804,821
39.	Percent of total production of oats[31, 35, 36]	. . .	. . .	. . .	. . .	. . .	24.6	28.9	36.5	56.6
40.	Production of soybeans in bushels[36, 40, 41]	. . .	. . .	. . .	. . .	. . .	. . .	. . .	. . .	. . .
41.	Percent of total production of soybeans[36, 40, 41]	. . .	. . .	. . .	. . .	. . .	. . .	. . .	. . .	. . .
42.	Production of hay crops in tons[31, 34, 42, 43, 44]	. . .	. . .	. . .	. . .	. . .	1,593,777	3,336,919	7,060,045	12,453,239
43.	Percent of total production of hay crops[31, 34, 40, 42, 43, 44]	. . .	. . .	. . .	. . .	. . .	15.6	24.1	37.0	45.6

b. Values in gold

c. Previous urban definition

d. Present urban definition

1880	1890	1900	1910	1920	1930	1940	1950	1960	1970
121.9	133.4	144.5	157.0	171.8	181.0	185.1	212.1	263.8	324.1
5,129,441,087	7,069,767,154	9,563,880,438	16,146,658,700	20,488,657,464	24,495,320,126	16,129,543,848	33,748,000,000	55,469,000,000	86,394,000,000
48.6	37.8	35.3	68.8	26.9	19.6	-34.1	109.2	64.4	55.8
3,021	3,675	4,354	7,267	9,391	11,781	7,692	18,065	37,974	75,002
1,350,225	1,474,086	1,583,841	1,567,990	1,477,942	1,355,007	1,343,417	1,410,195	1,142,639	976,295
772,457,900	1,195,704,262	1,576,977,350	2,528,038,019	3,866,514,280	3,044,413,966	2,128,926,747	5,598,540,708	7,296,637,722	9,106,980,000
455	622	718	1,138	1,772	1,464	1,015	2,996	4,995	7,906
329,550,755	321,316,830	338,504,885	410,742,889	625,328,899	476,014,472	409,354,000	606,935,000	576,429,333	768,760,000
71.7	68.6	67.1	73.9	66.1	59.5	57.7	59.5	54.6	56.1
1,285,284,661	1,598,870,008	1,941,220,100	1,841,657,282	1,578,970,240	1,544,439,135	1,725,969,715	2,208,064,240	3,449,080,000	3,568,800,000
73.2	75.3	72.8	72.2	67.3	72.5	74.7	79.5	80.6	87.0
270,166,435	645,127,344	764,279,166	806,464,050	827,815,804	861,928,754	699,649,034	978,097,183	807,704,134	734,637,000
66.2	79.7	81.0	80.1	78.5	86.8	80.4	86.1	80.7	80.8
...	...	...	...	...	6,311,949	82,860,507	188,415,798	389,065,426	734,637,000
...	...	...	...	...	72.9	94.6	88.7	75.5	80.8
19,182,478	41,010,825	41,696,731	51,790,848	48,697,466	45,949,000	41,255,425	45,613,558	56,936,060	63,266,000
54.6	61.4	58.6	59.4	53.9	53.9	50.1	51.2	53.4	49.6

53

General Statistics for Manufacturing Establishments by State[51,52]

	1899	1909	1919	1929	1939	1947	1954	1958	1963	1967	1971
ILLINOIS											
1. Total establishments (number)	14,374	18,026	17,808	15,333	11,983	15,993	17,628	18,468	18,593	18,536	
2. With 20 employees or more	NA	NA	NA	NA	NA	NA	6,377	6,586	6,974	7,477	
3. All employees, number (1,000)	373.8	543.7	785.9	827.5	752.7	1,186.1	1,222.4	1,189.9	1,211.2	1,397.3	1,282.2
4. Payroll ($1,000,000)	199.7	364.8	1,071.0	1,393.6	1,107.6	3,589.4	5,420.9	6,224.8	7,560.6	10,013.9	11,701.6
5. Production workers, total (number) (1,000)	332.9	465.8	650.0	691.6	591.0	955.1	903.0	835.2	855.9	995.1	871.2
6. Man-hours (1,000,000)	NA	NA	NA	NA	NA	NA	1,787.7	1,631.8	1,717.0	1,978.8	1,708.9
7. Wages ($1,000,000)	159.1	273.3	797.1	1,024.9	742.5	2,628.6	3,518.6	3,833.5	4,655.4	6,180.0	6,875.9
8. Value added by manufacture ($1,000,000)	439.4	758.4	1,929.1	2,930.0	2,187.2	6,683.1	9,663.8	11,664.1	14,641.5	20,016.5	22,789.8
9. Capital expenditures, new ($1,000,000)	NA	NA	NA	NA	NA	NA	551.7	730.7	775.6	1,493.4	1,476.3
10. Percent of U.S. employment	7.71	7.75	8.00	7.65	8.68	5.27	7.59	7.42	7.14	7.23	
11. Index of employment change (1958 = 100)	32	46	67	70	63	100	103	100	102	117	
12. U.S. index of employment change (1958 = 100)	30	44	61	60	59	89	100	100	106	121	
INDIANA											
1. Total establishments (number)	7,128	7,969	7,558	5,091	4,192	5,403	6,355	6,612	6,860	6,920	
2. With 20 employees or more	NA	NA	NA	NA	NA	NA	2,344	2,444	2,547	2,917	
3. All employees, number (1,000)	149.5	210.6	332.4	359.9	337.9	548.3	588.4	551.0	609.8	710.2	665.1
4. Payroll ($1,000,000)	69.3	121.8	400.9	534.2	474.1	1,582.8	2,533.4	2,874.7	3,794.3	5,023.2	6,003.1
5. Production workers, total (number) (1,000)	139.0	187.0	276.7	314.7	275.3	457.5	458.9	407.5	463.1	543.6	491.0
6. Man-hours (1,000,000)	NA	NA	NA	NA	NA	NA	904.1	796.0	937.2	1,078.1	957.4
7. Wages ($1,000,000)	59.3	95.5	316.0	418.8	342.7	1,232.2	1,798.8	1,912.8	2,622.1	3,453.5	3,957.9
8. Value added by manufacture ($1,000,000)	141.9	244.7	721.7	1,136.5	964.7	2,970.0	4,632.0	5,502.1	7,726.9	10,308.0	12,073.9
9. Capital expenditures, new ($1,000,000)	NA	NA	NA	NA	NA	NA	301.5	515.3	555.2	1,004.4	847.1
10. Percent of U.S. employment	3.08	3.00	3.38	3.73	3.55	3.83	3.65	3.44	3.60	3.68	
11. Index of employment change (1958 = 100)	27	38	60	65	61	99	106	100	111	129	
12. U.S. index of employment change (1958 = 100)	30	44	61	60	59	89	100	100	106	121	

General Statistics for Manufacturing Establishments by State[51, 52]

	1899	1909	1919	1929	1939	1947	1954	1958	1963	1967	1971
IOWA											
1. Total establishments (number)	4,828	5,528	5,104	3,317	2,541	2,963	3,320	3,596	3,496	3,388	
2. With 20 employees or more	NA	NA	NA	NA	NA	NA	881	945	982	1,092	
3. All employees, number (1,000)	49.6	73.0	98.5	97.4	88.1	140.4	163.7	166.1	178.2	210.1	200.8
4. Payroll ($1,000,000)	22.3	43.5	122.2	137.2	114.1	372.3	648.4	812.5	1,046.7	1,434.6	1,729.3
5. Production workers, total (number) (1,000)	44.4	61.6	79.2	81.7	64.8	112.5	122.8	120.7	126.9	154.0	143.2
6. Man-hours (1,000,000)	NA	NA	NA	NA	NA	NA	248.7	241.0	256.4	310.0	279.8
7. Wages ($1,000,000)	18.0	32.5	88.4	102.3	72.9	275.4	443.6	537.7	687.0	946.1	1,122.3
8. Value added by manufacture ($1,000,000)	47.1	88.5	221.8	323.8	243.4	671.0	1,236.0	1,684.3	2,287.0	3,250.9	3,941.1
9. Capital expenditures, new ($1,000,000)	NA	NA	NA	NA	NA	NA	73.4	103.2	127.0	230.7	262.6
10. Percent of U.S. employment	1.02	1.04	1.00	1.01	0.92	0.98	1.02	1.04	1.05	1.09	
11. Index of employment change (1958 = 100)	30	44	59	59	53	85	99	100	107	126	
12. U.S. index of employment change (1958 = 100)	30	44	61	60	59	89	100	100	106	121	
KANSAS											
1. Total establishments (number)	2,299	3,435	3,149	1,916	1,418	1,946	2,139	2,309	2,475	2,551	
2. With 20 employees or more	NA	NA	NA	NA	NA	NA	572	643	696	812	
3. All employees, number (1,000)	30.7	51.1	72.5	57.3	42.6	74.6	131.4	118.8	114.3	143.8	123.8
4. Payroll ($1,000,000)	15.9	33.3	93.6	85.2	56.4	204.8	560.5	590.8	684.4	964.8	1,019.3
5. Production workers, total (number) (1,000)	27.1	44.2	60.2	47.4	30.9	59.4	98.2	86.6	84.6	106.5	89.6
6. Man-hours (1,000,000)	NA	NA	NA	NA	NA	NA	203.1	173.9	176.9	218.1	175.5
7. Wages ($1,000,000)	12.8	25.9	71.8	63.3	36.1	151.3	400.6	403.7	463.2	655.4	669.2
8. Value added by manufacture ($1,000,000)	33.3	66.2	161.6	205.4	117.4	461.1	2,049.3	1,171.0	1,461.6	2,112.4	2,560.6
9. Capital expenditures, new ($1,000,000)	NA	NA	NA	NA	NA	NA	53.0	99.0	106.3	155.9	132.5
10. Percent of U.S. employment	0.63	0.73	0.74	0.59	0.45	0.52	0.82	0.74	0.67	0.74	
11. Index of employment change (1958 = 100)	26	43	61	48	36	63	111	100	96	121	
12. U.S. index of employment change (1958 = 100)	30	44	61	60	59	89	100	100	106	121	

General Statistics for Manufacturing Establishments by State[51, 52]

	1899	1909	1919	1929	1939	1947	1954	1958	1963	1967	1971
MICHIGAN											
1. Total establishments (number)	7,310	9,159	8,046	6,686	5,961	9,891	12,711	13,596	14,220	14,340	
2. With 20 employees or more	NA	NA	NA	NA	NA	NA	4,001	3,990	4,537	5,157	
3. All employees, number (1,000)	169.2	262.1	541.2	599.2	618.7	975.5	1,056.0	880.0	961.1	1,134.1	1,034.4
4. Payroll ($1,000,000)	74.9	153.8	787.2	1,041.8	1,025.0	3,097.3	5,248.9	5,161.2	6,950.7	9,357.2	11,128.6
5. Production workers, total (number) (1,000)	155.8	231.5	470.3	530.0	520.2	823.3	809.3	608.9	690.8	816.7	728.6
6. Man-hours (1,000,000)	NA	NA	NA	NA	NA	NA	1,650.3	1,204.1	1,473.9	1,669.2	1,463.5
7. Wages ($1,000,000)	62.5	119.0	638.4	840.5	788.0	2,444.6	3,661.0	3,184.8	4,521.0	6,008.0	6,965.4
8. Value added by manufacture ($1,000,000)	143.7	316.5	1,544.6	2,067.3	1,794.0	5,200.1	8,707.2	8,363.6	13,090.3	17,241.6	20,270.6
9. Capital expenditures, new ($1,000,000)	NA	NA	NA	NA	NA	NA	870.5	465.3	761.8	1,360.2	1,202.3
10. Percent of U.S. employment	3.49	3.74	5.50	6.20	6.49	6.82	6.56	5.49	5.67	5.87	
11. Index of employment change (1958 = 100)	19	30	61	68	70	111	120	100	109	129	
12. U.S. index of employment change (1958 = 100)	30	44	61	60	59	89	100	100	106	121	
MINNESOTA											
1. Total establishments (number)	4,096	5,561	5,633	4,315	3,735	4,563	5,027	5,380	5,500	5,409	
2. With 20 employees or more	NA	NA	NA	NA	NA	NA	1,316	1,433	1,587	1,778	
3. All employees, number (1,000)	71.2	99.0	140.4	124.2	102.2	181.5	208.5	220.8	245.9	299.8	277.5
4. Payroll ($1,000,000)	35.1	62.9	169.8	180.1	143.4	508.4	865.3	1,094.8	1,478.6	2,106.5	2,467.6
5. Production workers, total (number) (1,000)	64.6	84.8	113.8	103.4	78.0	145.0	151.1	149.6	165.6	198.8	177.3
6. Man-hours (1,000,000)	NA	NA	NA	NA	NA	NA	305.3	293.9	331.6	398.7	347.2
7. Wages ($1,000,000)	29.0	47.5	124.8	132.4	95.3	358.6	560.5	654.9	865.4	1,177.6	1,352.2
8. Value added by manufacture ($1,000,000)	73.4	127.8	327.9	405.0	306.8	1,021.3	1,594.5	2,050.4	2,806.1	4,080.2	4,827.2
9. Capital expenditures, new ($1,000,000)	NA	NA	NA	NA	NA	NA	82.2	108.5	159.1	231.3	271.1
10. Percent of U.S. employment	1.47	1.41	1.43	1.28	1.07	1.27	1.29	1.38	1.45	1.55	
11. Index of employment change (1958 = 100)	32	45	64	56	46	80	94	100	111	136	
12. U.S. index of employment change (1958 = 100)	30	44	61	60	59	89	100	100	106	121	

General Statistics for Manufacturing Establishments by State[51, 52]

	1899	1909	1919	1929	1939	1947	1954	1958	1963	1967	1971
MISSOURI											
1. Total establishments (number)	6,853	8,375	8,715	5,765	4,487	5,721	6,198	6,588	6,540	6,545	
2. With 20 employees or more	NA	NA	NA	NA	NA	NA	2,179	2,215	2,325	2,457	
3. All employees, number (1,000)	120.2	177.5	235.8	240.6	220.3	327.1	381.9	380.5	391.4	452.2	436.5
4. Payroll ($1,000,000)	60.0	109.8	273.7	332.3	280.7	826.2	1,496.7	1,771.1	2,235.2	3,048.9	3,673.2
5. Production workers, total (number) (1,000)	107.7	153.0	193.8	202.9	176.0	269.4	285.4	271.5	276.2	320.9	296.0
6. Man-hours (1,000,000)	NA	NA	NA	NA	NA	NA	552.7	519.3	547.8	631.3	569.5
7. Wages ($1,000,000)	46.7	80.8	194.9	240.4	187.5	606.8	977.3	1,088.7	1,361.7	1,851.7	2,135.0
8. Value added by manufacture ($1,000,000)	132.1	219.7	534.6	777.5	581.8	1,620.9	2,727.3	3,250.8	4,296.0	5,895.0	7,525.1
9. Capital expenditures, new ($1,000,000)	NA	NA	NA	NA	NA	NA	124.4	185.9	211.1	346.8	363.3
10. Percent of U.S. employment	2.48	2.53	2.40	2.49	2.31	2.29	2.38	2.37	2.31	2.34	
11. Index of employment change (1958 = 100)	32	47	62	63	58	86	97	100	103	119	
12. U.S. index of employment change (1958 = 100)	30	44	61	60	59	89	100	100	106	121	
NEBRASKA											
1. Total establishments (number)	1,695	2,500	2,385	1,491	1,093	1,341	1,423	1,553	1,611	1,672	
2. With 20 employees or more	NA	NA	NA	NA	NA	NA	378	412	474	525	
3. All employees, number (1,000)	21.0	29.4	44.9	34.8	26.2	47.0	59.4	58.6	64.9	77.0	80.2
4. Payroll ($1,000,000)	11.0	19.4	60.1	51.3	34.1	119.9	223.5	265.2	348.0	475.9	618.0
5. Production workers, total (number) (1,000)	18.7	24.3	35.4	28.2	18.4	37.3	43.4	42.9	47.0	58.4	58.7
6. Man-hours (1,000,000)	NA	NA	NA	NA	NA	NA	90.4	87.0	96.7	119.2	119.2
7. Wages ($1,000,000)	8.8	13.9	44.5	36.9	20.2	87.4	150.7	174.2	228.5	325.0	411.2
8. Value added by manufacture ($1,000,000)	34.3	47.9	112.6	120.0	68.1	260.6	394.2	536.3	746.6	1,150.0	1,594.1
9. Capital expenditures, new ($1,000,000)	NA	NA	NA	NA	NA	NA	36.4	49.9	46.1	71.4	86.5
10. Percent of U.S. employment	0.43	0.42	0.46	0.36	0.27	0.33	0.37	0.37	0.38	0.40	
11. Index of employment change (1958 = 100)	36	50	77	59	45	80	101	100	111	131	
12. U.S. index of employment change (1958 = 100)	30	44	61	60	59	89	100	100	106	121	

General Statistics for Manufacturing Establishments by State[51, 52]

	1899	1909	1919	1929	1939	1947	1954	1958	1963	1967	1971
NORTH DAKOTA											
1. Total establishments (number)	337	752	755	373	342	361	367	405	459	454	
2. With 20 employees or more	NA	NA	NA	NA	NA	NA	65	79	78	92	
3. All employees, number (1,000)	1.5	3.4	5.0	5.0	4.1	5.2	5.6	6.3	6.5	7.5	10.1
4. Payroll ($1,000,000)	0.8	2.4	6.4	7.8	5.0	12.3	19.2	26.3	31.5	41.6	70.3
5. Production workers, total (number) (1,000)	1.4	2.8	4.2	4.0	2.6	3.8	3.9	4.4	4.5	5.2	6.9
6. Man-hours (1,000,000)	NA	NA	NA	NA	NA	NA	8.3	8.8	9.1	10.7	14.5
7. Wages ($1,000,000)	0.7	1.8	5.0	5.7	2.7	8.5	12.5	17.0	19.8	26.1	42.9
8. Value added by manufacture ($1,000,000)	2.1	5.5	12.2	15.6	11.0	29.4	35.0	62.6	72.4	112.8	189.0
9. Capital expenditures, new ($1,000,000)	NA	NA	NA	NA	NA	NA	16.2	9.1	8.1	6.3	11.3
10. Percent of U.S. employment	0.03	0.05	0.05	0.05	0.04	0.04	0.03	0.04	0.04	0.04	
11. Index of employment change (1958 = 100)	24	54	79	79	64	82	89	100	103	119	
12. U.S. index of employment change (1958 = 100)	30	44	61	60	59	89	100	100	106	121	
OHIO											
1. Total establishments (number)	13,868	15,138	15,585	11,855	9,543	12,302	14,550	15,203	15,484	15,428	
2. With 20 employees or more	NA	NA	NA	NA	NA	NA	5,479	5,534	5,800	6,285	
3. All employees, number (1,000)	336.2	508.3	867.3	853.4	731.7	1,194.3	1,292.2	1,201.0	1,239.8	1,397.0	1,331.5
4. Payroll ($1,000,000)	164.6	317.6	1,214.6	1,404.2	1,120.8	3,559.5	5,821.0	6,522.5	8,125.4	10,523.1	12,512.9
5. Production workers, total (number) (1,000)	308.1	446.9	728.3	741.1	595.5	988.1	985.7	856.5	885.7	998.1	922.3
6. Man-hours (1,000,000)	NA	NA	NA	NA	NA	NA	1,946.8	1,658.5	1,799.7	2,014.5	1,819.3
7. Wages ($1,000,000)	136.4	245.5	941.3	1,102.2	809.4	2,727.0	4,015.3	4,170.2	5,257.2	6,745.4	7,796.1
8. Value added by manufacture ($1,000,000)	339.4	613.7	2,182.6	2,889.8	2,116.4	6,358.0	10,154.4	11,472.5	15,506.1	20,435.4	23,991.7
9. Capital expenditures, new ($1,000,000)	NA	NA	NA	NA	NA	NA	760.9	795.8	847.8	1,694.1	1,310.2
10. Percent of U.S. employment	6.93	7.25	8.82	8.83	7.68	8.36	8.02	7.50	7.31	7.23	
11. Index of employment change (1958 = 100)	28	42	72	71	61	99	108	100	103	116	
12. U.S. index of employment change (1958 = 100)	30	44	61	60	59	89	100	100	106	121	

General Statistics for Manufacturing Establishments by State[51, 52]

	1899	1909	1919	1929	1939	1947	1954	1958	1963	1967	1971
SOUTH DAKOTA											
1. Total establishments (number)	624	1,020	1,054	615	450	494	546	575	586	604	
2. With 20 employees or more	NA	NA	NA	NA	NA	87	92	109	115	137	
3. All employees, number (1,000)	2.5	4.3	6.8	7.8	7.3	10.3	11.5	12.9	13.2	15.5	16.1
4. Payroll ($1,000,000)	1.3	2.9	8.8	10.7	9.0	25.8	41.1	54.8	70.0	92.5	118.8
5. Production workers, total (number) (1,000)	2.2	3.6	5.6	6.5	5.4	8.1	8.4	9.6	9.6	11.3	11.3
6. Man-hours (1,000,000)	NA	NA	NA	NA	NA	17.7	18.0	18.6	19.9	22.4	22.5
7. Wages ($1,000,000)	1.1	2.3	6.8	8.1	5.9	19.2	28.0	37.5	48.0	61.7	78.4
8. Value added by manufacture ($1,000,000)	3.0	6.4	17.1	22.7	19.6	51.4	77.7	114.3	140.0	171.3	226.2
9. Capital expenditures, new ($1,000,000)	NA	NA	NA	NA	NA	3.4	3.4	5.2	7.3	8.2	13.5
10. Percent of U.S. employment	0.05	0.06	0.07	0.08	0.08	0.07	0.07	0.08	0.08	0.08	
11. Index of employment change (1958 = 100)	19	33	53	60	57	80	89	100	102	120	
12. U.S. index of employment change (1958 = 100)	30	44	61	60	59	89	100	100	106	121	
WISCONSIN											
1. Total establishments (number)	7,841	9,721	9,720	7,431	6,334	6,980	7,702	7,890	7,937	7,838	
2. With 20 employees or more	NA	NA	NA	NA	NA	NA	2,294	2,331	2,467	2,727	
3. All employees, number (1,000)	148.0	204.9	308.0	309.4	251.8	418.7	439.2	439.4	461.8	512.2	479.8
4. Payroll ($1,000,000)	66.2	119.6	375.7	467.5	364.6	1,190.8	1,869.1	2,208.9	2,781.1	3,577.8	4,227.1
5. Production workers, total (number) (1,000)	137.5	182.6	262.2	264.7	198.6	343.9	332.3	320.0	338.5	374.5	342.2
6. Man-hours (1,000,000)	NA	NA	NA	NA	NA	NA	669.3	634.1	687.8	754.8	670.2
7. Wages ($1,000,000)	55.7	93.9	288.7	352.5	249.9	908.2	1,268.6	1,440.4	1,827.4	2,332.8	2,681.7
8. Value added by manufacture ($1,000,000)	141.1	243.9	715.8	949.8	682.0	2,263.0	3,334.0	3,959.5	5,363.2	7,014.1	8,476.4
9. Capital expenditures, new ($1,000,000)	NA	NA	NA	NA	NA	NA	169.4	203.7	280.7	506.6	406.4
10. Percent of U.S. employment	3.05	2.92	3.13	3.20	2.64	2.93	2.73	2.74	2.72	2.65	
11. Index of employment change (1958 = 100)	34	47	70	70	57	95	100	100	105	117	
12. U.S. index of employment change (1958 = 100)	30	44	61	60	59	89	100	100	106	121	

General Statistics for Manufacturing Establishments by State[51, 52]

	1899	1909	1919	1929	1939	1947	1954	1958	1963	1967	1971
				MIDWEST REGIONAL TOTALS							
1. Total establishments (number)	71,253	87,184	84,972	64,188	52,079	67,958	77,966	82,175	83,761	83,685	
2. With 20 employees or more	NA	NA	NA	NA	NA	NA	25,978	26,721	28,582	31,456	
3. All employees, number (1,000)	1,473.4	2,167.3	3,438.5	3,516.6	3,183.5	5,108.9	5,560.3	5,225.3	5,498.1	6,356.7	5,938.0
4. Payroll ($1,000,000)	720.8	1,352.0	4,584.0	5,646.0	4,734.8	15,089.5	24,747.9	27,607.6	35,106.5	46,660.0	55,269.8
5. Production workers, total (number) (1,000)	1,339.4	1,888.1	2,879.6	3,016.3	2,556.8	4,203.3	4,202.4	3,713.6	3,948.4	4,583.2	4,138.3
6. Man-hours (1,000,000)	NA	NA	NA	NA	NA	NA	8,384.7	7,267.0	8,054.0	9,205.6	8,147.5
7. Wages ($1,000,000)	590.2	1,032.0	3,517.5	4,328.0	3,353.0	11,447.7	16,835.6	17,455.4	22,556.7	29,763.3	34,088.1
8. Value added by manufacture ($1,000,000)	1,530.9	2,739.2	8,481.6	11,843.5	9,092.6	27,589.9	43,605.3	49,831.5	68,137.7	91,788.2	108,465.8
9. Capital expenditures, new ($1,000,000)	NA	NA	NA	NA	NA	2,204.0	3,043.0	3,271.6	3,886.1	7,109.2	6,383.1
10. Percent of U.S. employment	30.38	30.91	34.95	36.40	33.41	35.74	34.54	32.61	32.42	32.90	
11. Index of employment change (1958 = 100)	29.5	43	64.5	64	57	91.5	104	100	105	123	
12. U.S. index of employment change (1958 = 100)	30	44	61	60	59	89	100	100	106	121	

Population of Cities Having 50,000 Inhabitants or More in 1950[53, 54]

1900 to 1970

	1900	1910	1920	1930	1940	1950	1960	1970
Akron, Ohio	42,728	69,067	208,435	255,040	244,791	274,605	290,351	275,425
Aurora, Ill.	24,147	29,807	36,397	46,589	47,170	50,576	63,715	74,182
Bay City, Mich.	27,628	45,166	47,554	47,355	47,956	52,523	53,604	49,449
Berwyn, Ill.	———	5,841	14,150	47,027	48,451	51,280	54,224	52,502
Canton, Ohio	30,667	50,217	87,091	104,906	108,401	116,912	113,631	110,053
Cedar Rapids, Iowa	25,656	32,811	45,566	56,097	62,120	72,296	92,035	110,642
Chicago, Ill.	1,698,575	2,185,283	2,701,705	3,376,438	3,396,808	3,620,962	3,550,404	3,366,957
Cicero, Ill.	16,310	14,557	44,995	66,602	64,712	67,544	69,130	67,058
Cincinnati, Ohio	325,902	363,591	401,247	451,160	455,610	503,998	502,550	452,524
Cleveland, Ohio	381,768	560,663	796,841	900,429	878,336	914,808	876,050	750,903
Cleveland Hgts., Ohio	———	2,955	15,236	50,945	54,992	59,141	61,813	60,767
Columbus, Ohio	125,560	181,511	237,031	290,564	306,087	375,901	471,316	539,677
Davenport, Iowa	35,254	43,028	56,727	60,751	66,039	74,549	88,981	98,469
Dayton, Ohio	85,333	116,577	152,559	200,982	210,718	243,872	262,332	243,601
Dearborn, Mich.	844	911	2,470	50,358	63,584	94,994	112,007	104,199
Decatur, Ill.	20,754	31,140	43,818	57,510	59,305	66,269	78,004	90,397
Des Moines, Iowa	62,139	86,368	126,468	142,559	159,819	177,965	208,982	200,587
Detroit, Mich.	285,704	465,766	993,678	1,568,662	1,623,452	1,849,568	1,670,144	1,511,482
Duluth, Minn.	52,969	78,466	98,917	101,463	101,065	104,511	106,884	100,578
East Chicago, Ind.	3,411	19,098	35,967	54,784	54,637	54,263	57,669	46,982
East St. Louis, Ill.	29,655	58,547	66,767	74,347	75,609	82,295	81,712	69,996
Evanston, Ill.	19,259	24,978	37,234	63,338	65,389	73,641	79,283	79,808
Evansville, Ind.	59,007	69,647	85,264	102,249	97,062	128,636	141,543	138,764
Flint, Mich.	13,103	38,550	91,599	156,492	151,543	163,143	196,940	193,317
Fort Wayne, Ind.	45,115	63,933	86,549	114,946	118,410	133,607	161,776	177,671
Gary, Ind.	———	16,802	55,378	100,426	111,719	133,911	178,320	175,415
Grand Rapids, Mich.	87,565	112,571	137,634	168,592	164,292	176,313	177,313	197,649
Green Bay, Wis.	18,684	25,236	31,017	37,415	46,235	52,735	62,888	87,809
Hamilton, Ohio	23,914	35,279	39,675	52,176	50,592	57,951	72,354	67,865
Hammond, Ind.	12,376	20,925	36,004	64,560	70,184	87,594	111,698	107,790
Indianapolis, Ind.	169,164	233,650	314,194	364,161	386,972	427,173	476,258	744,624
Jackson, Mich.	25,180	31,433	48,374	55,187	49,656	51,088	50,720	45,484
Joliet, Ill.	29,353	34,670	38,442	42,993	42,365	51,601	66,780	80,378
Kalamazoo, Mich.	24,404	39,437	48,487	54,786	54,097	57,704	82,089	85,555

Population of Cities Having 50,000 Inhabitants or More in 1950 (Cont.)

1900 to 1970

	1900	1910	1920	1930	1940	1950	1960	1970
Kansas City, Kans.	51,418	82,331	101,177	121,857	121,458	129,553	121,901	168,213
Kansas City, Mo.	163,752	248,381	324,410	399,746	399,178	456,622	475,539	507,087
Kenosha, Wis.	11,606	21,371	40,472	50,262	48,765	54,368	67,899	78,805
Lakewood, Ohio	3,355	15,181	41,732	70,509	69,160	68,071	66,154	70,173
Lansing, Mich.	16,485	31,229	57,327	78,397	78,753	92,129	107,807	131,546
Lima, Ohio	21,723	30,508	41,326	42,287	44,711	50,246	51,037	53,734
Lincoln, Nebr.	40,169	43,973	54,948	75,933	81,984	98,884	128,521	149,518
Lorain, Ohio	16,028	28,883	37,295	44,512	44,125	51,202	68,932	78,185
Madison, Wis.	19,164	25,531	38,378	57,899	67,447	96,056	126,706	173,258
Milwaukee, Wis.	285,315	373,857	457,147	578,249	587,472	637,392	741,324	717,099
Minneapolis, Minn.	202,718	301,408	380,582	464,356	492,370	521,718	482,872	434,400
Muncie, Ind.	20,942	24,005	36,524	46,548	49,720	58,479	68,603	69,080
Oak Park, Ill.	———	19,444	39,858	63,982	66,015	63,529	61,093	62,511
Omaha, Nebr.	102,555	124,096	191,601	214,006	223,844	251,117	301,598	347,328
Peoria, Ill.	56,100	66,950	76,121	104,969	105,087	111,856	103,162	126,963
Pontiac, Mich.	9,769	14,532	34,273	64,928	66,626	73,681	82,233	85,279
Racine, Wis.	29,102	38,002	58,593	67,542	67,195	71,193	89,144	95,162
Rockford, Ill.	31,051	45,401	65,651	85,864	84,637	92,927	126,706	147,370
Saginaw, Mich.	42,345	50,510	61,903	80,715	82,794	92,918	98,265	91,849
St. Joseph, Mo.	102,979	77,403	77,939	80,935	75,711	78,588	79,673	72,691
St. Louis, Mo.	575,238	687,029	772,897	821,960	816,048	856,796	750,026	622,236
St. Paul, Minn.	163,065	214,744	234,698	271,606	287,736	311,349	313,411	309,980
Sioux City, Iowa	33,111	47,828	71,227	79,183	82,364	83,991	89,159	85,925
Sioux Falls, S. Dak.	———	14,094	25,202	33,362	40,832	52,696	65,466	72,488
South Bend, Ind.	35,999	53,684	70,983	104,268	101,268	115,911	132,445	125,580
Springfield, Ill.	34,159	51,678	59,183	71,864	75,503	81,628	83,271	91,753
Springfield, Mo.	23,267	35,201	39,631	57,527	61,238	66,731	95,865	120,096
Springfield, Ohio	38,253	46,921	60,840	68,743	70,662	78,508	82,723	81,926
Terre Haute, Ind.	36,673	58,157	66,083	62,810	62,693	64,214	72,500	70,286
Toledo, Ohio	131,822	168,497	243,164	290,718	282,349	303,616	318,003	383,818
Topeka, Kans.	33,608	43,684	50,022	64,120	67,833	78,791	119,484	125,011
Waterloo, Iowa	12,580	26,693	36,230	46,191	51,743	65,198	71,755	75,533
Wichita, Kans.	24,671	52,450	72,217	111,110	114,966	168,279	254,698	276,554
Youngstown, Ohio	44,885	79,066	132,358	170,002	167,720	168,330	166,689	139,788

NOTES

1. U.S. Bureau of the Census. *U.S. Census of Population: 1970,* Volume I, Part 1, Sec. 1, pp. 48-49.

2. U.S. Bureau of the Census. *U.S. Census of Population: 1970,* Volume I, Part 1, pp. 1-50.

3. U.S. Bureau of the Census. *Twelfth Census of the U.S.: 1900,* Volume 1, Part 1, pp. 4-5.

4. U.S. Bureau of the Census. *U.S. Census of Population: 1970,* Volume I, Part 1, pp. 1-51.

5. U.S. Bureau of the Census. *U.S. Census of Population: 1970,* Volume I, Part 1, pp. 1-52.

6. U.S. Bureau of the Census. *Statistical Abstract of the U.S.: 1940,* p. 6.

7. U.S. Bureau of the Census. *U.S. Census of Population: 1970,* Volume I, Part 1, pp. 1-53.

8. U.S. Bureau of the Census. *Negro Population 1790-1915* (1918), pp. 44-45.

9. U.S. Bureau of the Census. *Statistical Abstract of the U.S.: 1942,* pp. 12-13.

10. U.S. Bureau of the Census. *Statistical Abstract of the U.S.: 1972,* p. 28.

11. U.S. Bureau of the Census. *Twelfth Census of the U.S.- 1900, Special Reports of the Census Office, Supplementary Analysis,* pp. 242-246.

12. U.S. Bureau of the Census. *Abstract of the Fourteenth Census of the U.S.: 1920,* p. 105.

13. U.S. Bureau of the Census. *Abstract of the Fifteenth Census of the U.S.: 1930,* p. 89.

14. U.S. Bureau of the Census. *Fifteenth Census of the U.S.: 1930,* Volume II, *Population,* p. 38.

15. U.S. Bureau of the Census, *Statistical Abstract of the U.S.: 1972,* p. 28.

16. U.S. Bureau of the Census. *A Century of Population Growth in the U.S. 1790-1900,* p. 133.

17. U.S. Bureau of the Census. *U.S. Census of the Population: 1970,* Volume I, Part 1, Sec. 1, pp. 62-71.

18. U.S. Bureau of the Census. *U.S. Census of Agriculture: 1959,* Volume II, *General Report, Statistics by Subject,* pp. 53-64.

19. U.S. Bureau of the Census. *U.S. Census of Agriculture: 1969,* Volume II, *General Report,* pp. 21-27, 64.

20. U.S. Bureau of the Census. *Abstract of the Fourteenth Census of the U.S.: 1920,* pp. 590-599.

21. U.S. Bureau of the Census. *Twelfth Census of the U.S. Taken in the Year 1900, Agriculture,* Part 1, pp. 688-689.

22. U.S. Bureau of the Census. *Abstract of the Fourteenth Census of the U.S.: 1920,* p. 630.

23. U.S. Bureau of the Census. *Statistical Abstract of the U.S.: 1940,* pp. 644-645.

24. U.S. Bureau of the Census. *Statistical Abstract of the U.S.: 1941,* pp. 682-683.

25. U.S. Bureau of the Census. *Statistical Abstract of the U.S.: 1960,* p. 628.

26. U.S. Bureau of the Census. *Statistical Abstract of the U.S.: 1962,* p. 619.

27. U.S. Bureau of the Census. *1969 Census of Agriculture,* Volume II, *General Report,* pp. 23-24.

28. U.S. Bureau of the Census. *Twelfth Census of the U.S. Taken in the Year 1900, Agriculture,* Part 1, pp. 700-701.

29. U.S. Bureau of the Census. *Abstract of the Fourteenth Census of the U.S.: 1920,* pp. 752-753.

30. U.S. Bureau of the Census. *U.S. Census of Agriculture: 1959,* Volume II, *General Report, Statistics by Subject,* p. 497.

31. U.S. Bureau of the Census. *U.S. Census of Agriculture: 1945,* Volume II, *General Report, Statistics by Subject,* pp. 466-467, 474-475, 496.

32. U.S. Bureau of the Census. *Statistical Abstract of the U.S.: 1952,* p. 621.

33. U.S. Bureau of the Census. *U.S. Census of Agriculture: 1909 and 1910,* pp. 591, 592, 601, 641.

34. U.S. Bureau of the Census. *Sixteenth Census of the U.S. 1940, Agriculture,* Volume III, pp. 780-781.

35. U.S. Bureau of the Census. *U.S. Census of Agriculture: 1959, General Report, Statistics by Subjects,* pp. 722-723, 740-741.

36. U.S. Department of Agriculture. *Agricultural Statistics 1972,* pp. 2-4, 36, 44-45, 76, 125, 162-163, 320, 359, 398-399, 506-509, 564-565.

37. U.S. Bureau of the Census. *Twelfth Census of the U.S. Taken in the Year 1900,* Volume VI, *Agriculture,* Part 2, pp. 80-81.

38. U.S. Bureau of the Census. *U.S. Census of Agriculture: 1959,* Volume II, *General Report, Statistics by Subject,* pp. 706-707.

39. U.S. Bureau of the Census. *Statistical Abstract of the U.S.: 1961,* p. 658.

40. U.S. Bureau of the Census. *U.S. Census of Agriculture: 1930,* p. 770.

41. U.S. Bureau of the Census. *U.S. Census of Agriculture: 1959, General Report, Statistics by Subjects,* pp. 770-771.

42. U.S. Bureau of the Census. *Eleventh Census of the U.S. Taken in the Year 1890, Agriculture,* pp. 95-98.

43. U.S. Bureau of the Census. *U.S. Census of Agriculture: 1959,* Volume II, *General Report, Statistics by Subject,* pp. 792-793.

44. U.S. Bureau of the Census. *Fourteenth Census of the U.S. 1920,* Volume V, *Agriculture,* pp. 794-795, 818.

45. U.S. Bureau of the Census. *Twelfth Census of the U.S. Taken in the Year 1900,* Volume VIII, Part 2, pp. 982-989.

46. U.S. Bureau of the Census. *Abstract of the Fourteenth Census of the U.S.: 1920,* pp. 1168-1171.

47. U.S. Bureau of the Census. *Abstract of the Fifteenth Census of the U.S.: 1930,* pp. 758-759.

48. U.S. Bureau of the Census. *Statistical Abstract of the U.S.: 1941,* pp. 878-881.

49. U.S. Bureau of the Census. *Sixteenth Census of the U.S. 1940, Agriculture,* Volume III, p. 51.

50. U.S. Bureau of the Census. *Thirteenth Census of the U.S. 1910,* Volume V, *Agriculture,* pp. 67-75.

51. U.S. Bureau of the Census. *1967 Census of Manufactures,* Volume I, *Summary and Subject Statistics,* pp. 62-80.

52. U.S. Bureau of the Census. *Annual Survey of Manufactures: 1971.* Parts 3 and 4.

53. U.S. Bureau of the Census. *Statistical Abstract of the U.S.: 1960,* pp. 18-21.

54. U.S. Bureau of the Census. *1970 Census of Population,* Volume I, Part 1, pp. 121-170.

White and Non-White Population: The classification of the population by color is not ordinarily based on replies to census questions asked by the enumerators but rather is obtained by observation. This concept does not, therefore, reflect a clear-cut definition of biological stock. The non-white population consists of Negroes, American Indians, Japanese, Chinese, Filipinos, and some other groups. Persons of mixed parentage are placed in the color classification of the non-white parent. Persons of Mexican birth or ancestry who are not definitely Indian or of other non-white stock have been classified as white in all censuses except that of 1930. In the 1930 Census, Mexicans were classified as non-white.[1]

1970 Racial Definition: The concept of race as used by the Bureau of the Census in 1970 reflects self-identification by respondents. The 1970 census obtained information on race primarily through self-enumeration; the data represent essentially self-classification by people according to the race with which they identify themselves.

For persons of mixed parentage who were in doubt as to their classification, the race of the person's father was used. In 1960, persons who reported mixed parentage of white and any other race were classified according to the other race; mixtures of races other than white were classified according to the race of the father.

The category "white" includes persons who indicated their race as white, as well as persons who did not classify themselves in one of the specific race categories on the questionnaire but entered Mexican, Puerto Rican, or a response suggesting Indo-European stock.

The category "Negro" includes persons who indicated their race as Negro or Black, as well as persons who did not classify themselves in one of the specific race categories on the questionnaire, but who had such entires as Jamaican, Trinidadian, West Indian, Haitian, and Ethiopian. The term "Negro and other races" includes persons of all races other than white.[2]

Urban/Rural Population: According to the definition adopted for use in the 1960 Census, the urban population comprises all persons living in (a) places of 2,500 inhabitants or more incorporated as cities, boroughs, villages, and towns (except towns in New England, New York and Wisconsin); (b) the densely settled urban fringe, whether incorporated or unincorporated, or urbanized areas; (c) towns in New England and townships in New Jersey and Pennsylvania which contain no incorporated municipalities as subdivisions and have either 25,000 inhabitants or more or a population of 2,500 to 25,000 and a density of 1,500 persons or more to a square mile; (d) counties in states other than the New England States, New Jersey and Pennsylvania that have no incorporated municipalities within their boundaries and have a density of 1,500 persons per square mile; and (e) unincorporated places of 2,500 inhabitants or more. In other words, the urban population comprises all persons living in urbanized areas and in places of 2,500 inhabitants or more outside urbanized areas. The population not classified as urban constitutes the rural population.

Substantially the same definition was used in the 1950 Census, the difference being confined to the urban towns in New England and to urban townships in New Jersey and Pennsylvania. In censuses prior to 1950, the urban population comprises all persons living in incorporated places of 2,500 inhabitants or more and areas (usually minor civil divisions) classified as urban under somewhat different special rules relating to population size and density.[3]

1970 Urban Definition: The 1970 criteria are essentially the same as those used in 1960 with two exceptions. The extended city concept is new for 1970. Secondly, in 1960, towns in the New England States, townships in New Jersey and Pennsylvania, and counties elsewhere, which were classified as urban in accordance with specific criteria, were included in the contiguous urbanized areas. In 1970 only those portions of towns and townships in these States that met the rules followed in defining urbanized areas elsewhere in the United States are included.

Extended cities. — Over the 1960-1970 decade there has been an increasing trend toward the extension of city boundaries to include

---

1. Bureau of the Census, *Historical Statistics of the United States, Colonial Times to 1957,* pp. 2 and 9.
2. Bureau of the Census, *Census of Population: 1970,* Vol. I, Pt. 2, Appendix B, p. 8.

3. Bureau of the Census, *Census of Population: 1960,* Vol. I, Pt. A, p. xii.

territory essentially rural in character. Examples are city-county consolidations such as the creation of the city of Chesapeake, Va., from South Norfolk City and Norfolk County and the extension of Oklahoma City, Okla., into five counties. The classification of all the inhabitants of such cities as urban would include in the urban population persons whose environment is primarily rural in character. In order to separate these people from those residing in the closely settled portions of such cities, the Bureau of the Census examined patterns of population density and classified a portion or portions of each such city as rural. An extended city contains one or more areas, each of at least 5 square miles in extent and with a population density of less than 100 persons per square mile according to the 1970 census. The area or areas constitute at least 25 percent of the land area of the legal city or total 25 square miles or more.

These cities—designated as extended cities—thus consist of an urban part and a rural part. When an extended city is a central city of an urbanized area or a standard metropolitan statistical area, only the urban part is considered as the central city. If the extended city is shown separately under the area, the city name is followed by the term "urban part." In tables in which the city name is not followed by this term, the population figure shown is for the entire city.[4]
Farm: For the 1958 Census of Agriculture, the definition of a farm was based primarily on a combination of "acres in the place" and the estimated value of agriculture sold.

The word "place" was defined to include all land under the control or supervision of one person or partnership at the time of enumeration and on which agricultural operations were conducted at any time in 1959.

Places of 10 or more acres in 1959 were counted as farms if the estimated sale of agricultural products for the year amounted to at least $50. Places of less than 10 acres in 1959 were counted as farms if the estimated sales of agricultural products for the year amounted to at least $250. Places not meeting the minimum estimated level of sales in 1959 were nevertheless counted as farms if they could normally be expected to produce agricultural products in sufficient quantity to meet the requirements of the definition.

In 1950 agricultural operations were defined to include every place of three or more acres, whether or not the operator considered it a farm, and every place having "specialized operations," regardless of the acreage. "Specialized operations" referred to nurseries and greenhouses and to places having 100 or more poultry, production of 300 or more dozen eggs in 1949, or 3 or more hives of bees.

For the 1950 Census of Agriculture, places of 3 or more acres were counted as farms if the annual value of agricultural products, whether for home use or for sale but exclusive of home-garden products, amounted to $150 or more. Places of less than 3 acres were counted as farms only if the annual sales of agricultural products amounted to $150 or more. A few places with very low agricultural production because of unusual circumstances, such as crop failures, were also counted as farms if they normally could have been expected to meet the minimum value or sales criteria. The decrease in the number of farms in 1950 and 1959, as compared with earlier censuses, was partly due to changes in the farm definition, especially with respect to places of 3 or more acres in size.

The definition of a census farm has been changed several times since 1850. However in all censuses, the essential features of the farm definition have been that: (1) the land should be under the control of one person and (2) that the land should be used for or connected with agricultural operations.

The requirement that the tracts of land be operated by one person has resulted in the counting of places operated by tenants, sharecroppers, and managers as separate farms. The requirement that all tracts operated by one person be considered one farm resulted in counting as one farm, places comprising owned land and rented land, and tracts of land operated by one person but widely separated as to location.

Agricultural operations have been considered to include the growing of crops; the raising of domestic animals, poultry, and bees; and the production of other agricultural products, including the production of livestock on public lands and open ranges not under the exclusive control of a single individual.

4. Bureau of the Census, *Census of Population: 1970,* Vol. I, Pt. 2, Appendix A, pp. 2, 5.

MINIMUM CRITERIA FOR CENSUS FARMS OF 3 OR MORE ACRES:

CENSUSES OF 1850 to 1959[5]

Census year	Minimum value of agricultural products produced for home use or for sale (dollars)	Minimum value of agricultural products sold (dollars)	Other criteria	Reduction in number of farms because of change in definition
1959[1]	Not applied	50	None	232,000
1954	150	Not applied	None	160,000
1950	150	Not applied	None	
1945	150[2]	Not applied	Agricultural operations comprising 3 or more acres of cropland or pastureland	
1940	Not applied	Not applied	Agricultural operations	
1935	Not applied	Not applied	Agricultural operations	
1930	Not applied	Not applied	Agricultural operations	
1925	Not applied	Not applied	Agricultural operations	
1920	Not applied	Not applied	Agricultural operations	
1910	Not applied	Not applied	Agricultural operations	
1900	Not applied	Not applied	Agricultural operations and continuous services of at least 1 person	
1890	Not applied	Not applied	Agricultural operations	
1880	Not applied	Not applied	Agricultural operations	
1870	Not applied	Not applied	Agricultural operations	
1860	100	Not applied	None	
1850	100	Not applied	None	

1. The minimum size criteria for 1959 applied to places of 10 or more acres.
2. Applied only if farm had less than 3 acres of cropland and pasture.

MINIMUM CRITERIA FOR CENSUS FARMS OF LESS THAN 3 ACRES:

CENSUSES OF 1850 to 1959[5]

Census year	Minimum value of agricultural products produced for home use or for sale (dollars)	Minimum value of agricultural products sold (dollars)	Other criteria	Index number of prices received by farmers (1910-1914 = 100)	Number of farms of less than 3 acres
1959	Not applied	250[1]	None	240	79,000
1954	Not applied	150	None	249	100,000
1950	Not applied	150	None	250	77,000
1945	250	Not applied	None	197	99,000
1940	250	Not applied	None	95	36,000
1935	250	Not applied	None	90	36,000
1930	250	Not applied	None	148	43,000
1925	250	Not applied	None	143	15,000
1920	250[2]	Not applied	None	217	20,000
1910	250[2]	Not applied	None	104	18,000
1900	Not applied	Not applied	Constant services of at least 1 person	NA	41,000
1890	Not applied	500	None	NA	NA
1880	Not applied	500	None	NA	4,000
1870	Not applied	500	None	NA	NA
1860	100	Not applied	None	NA	NA
1850	100	Not applied	None	NA	NA

NA — Not available.

1. The minimum size criteria for 1959 applied to places of less than 10 acres.
2. Not applicable when farm required services of at least 1 person.

5. Bureau of Census. *Census of Agriculture: 1959,* Vol. II, General Report, Statistics by Subjects, pp. xxvi-xxvii.

Improved Land: This category includes all land regularly tilled or mowed, land in pasture which has been cleared or tilled, land lying fallow, land in gardens, orchards, vineyards, and nurseries, and land occupied by farm buildings. Substantially the same classification of farm land has been employed at different censuses beginning with 1880. However, in 1920 the definition called for the inclusion as improved land of all pasture land which **had been cleared or tilled**, while in 1910 the only pasture land included as improved land was land **pastured and cropped in rotation**. This change in definition resulted in only a very limited change.[6]

Cropland Harvested: This includes land from which crops were harvested, land from which hay (including wild hay) was cut, and land in small fruits, orchards, vineyards, nurseries, and greenhouses. Land from which two or more crops were harvested was to be counted only once.

Figures for cropland harvested relate to the crop years immediately preceding the Census date; other data relate to the Census date: October and November for 1959; April 1 for 1950, 1940, and 1930; January 1 for 1920; April 15 for 1910; June 1 for earlier censuses.[7]

Farm Population: Farm population figures relate to the civilian population living on farms, regardless of occupation or source of incomes. The determination of whether a household is located on a farm has been made largely by the residents themselves. If the respondent in reply to the inquiry, "Is this house a farm (or ranch)?" answers affirmatively, it is, in most cases, classified as a farm dwelling unit and the occupants as part of the farm population. Excluded are the following: persons living on farmland who rent for cash a home and yard only; persons in summer camps, motels, and tourist camps; and persons in institutions on farmland.[8]

Manufacturing Establishments: The Censuses of 1850 to 1920 use the term "manufacturing establishment" to designate factories or plants whose products were valued at $500 or more, but in 1930 and 1940 the minimum limit was $5,000.[9] Beginning with the 1947 manufacturing census, reports were required from all establishments employing one or more persons at any time during the census year. This change in the minimum size limit in 1947 has not appreciably affected the historical comparability of earlier census figures except for data on number of establishments for a few industries.[10]

Capital: The form of the inquiry regarding capital, at all censuses from 1850 to and including 1880, was so vague and general in its character that it cannot be assumed that any true proportion exists between the statistics on this subject as elicited prior to 1890.[11]

The censuses from 1890 through 1920 contain data on capital which was compiled on the basis of more specific instructions; however, its value is limited to comparisons of very general conditions.[12]

At the Census of 1880, the question on capital read: "Capital (real and personal) invested in the business." At the Census of 1890, live capital, i.e., cash on hand, bills receivable, unsettled ledger accounts, raw materials, stock in process of manufacture, finished products on hand, and other sundries, was for the first time included as a separate and distinct item of capital, and the capital invested in realty was divided between land, buildings, and machinery. The form of inquiry in 1890 and 1900 was so similar that comparison may safely be made.[13]

In the Censuses of 1910 through 1920, the instructions for securing data relating to capital were as follows: "The answer should show the total amount of capital, both owned and borrowed, on the last day of the business year reported. All the items of fixed and live capital may be taken at the amounts carried on the books. If land or buildings are rented, that fact should be stated and no value given. If a part of the land or buildings is owned, the remainder being rented, that fact should be so stated and only the value of the owned

---

6. Bureau of Census. *Fourteenth Census of the United States: 1920,* Vol. V, Agriculture, p. 17.
7. Bureau of Census. *Census of Agriculture: 1959,* Vol. II, General Report, Statistics by Subjects, pp. 6, 58-64.
8. Bureau of the Census. *Historical Statistics of the U.S., Colonial Times to 1957,* p. 40.

9. Bureau of Census. *Statistical Abstract: 1942,* p. 885.
10. Bureau of Census. *Census of Manufactures: 1963,* Vol. 1, pp. 5-9.
11. Bureau of Census. *Twelfth Census of the United States: 1900,* Vol. VIII, Pt. II, p. viii.
12. Bureau of Census. *Fourteenth Census of the United States: 1920,* Vol. IX, p. 17.
13. Bureau of the Census. *Twelfth Census of the United States: 1900,* Vol. VIII, Pt. II, p. viii.

property given. Do not include securities and loans representing investments in other enterprises."[14] After the Census of 1920, this item was discontinued.

Average number of Wage Earners: At the censuses of 1850, 1860, and 1870, the inquiries regarding employees called for "average number of hands employed." The inquiries of 1880 were similar. In the Census of 1890 the average number of persons employed during the entire year was called for; and the average number was computed for the actual time the establishments were reported as being in operation. At the census of 1900 the greatest and least numbers of employees were reported, and also the average number employed during each month of the year. The average number of wage earners (men, women, and children) employed during the entire year was computed in the Census office by using 12, the number of calendar months, as a divisor into the total of the average numbers reported for each month. This difference in the method of ascertaining the average number of wage-earners during the entire year has resulted in a variation in the average number as between these two censuses, and should be considered in making comparisons.

The schedules for 1890 included in the wage-earning class "overseers and foremen or superintendents (not general superintendents or managers)," while the census of 1900 separated from the wage-earning class such salaried employees as general superintendents, clerks, and salesmen. Therefore this item varies in exactness.[15]

In the census of 1900, persons engaged in manufacturing were shown as (1) Proprietors and firm members, (2) Salaried officials, clerks, etc., and (3) Wage earners. In the Census of 1910 the following categories were used: (1) Proprietors and firm members, not including the stockholders of incorporated companies or the members of cooperative associations; (2) Salaried officials of corporations; (3) Superintendents, (4) Managers, clerks, and other salaried employees; (5) Wage earners including pieceworkers. Further inquiry in regard to wage earners called for the number employed on the 15th of each month.[16]

The Census of 1920 continued the foregoing categories of employees except that it included superintendents in one category.

As in 1900 and 1910, the average number of wage earners was computed by dividing the sum of the numbers reported for the several months by 12.[17]

The Census of 1930 made a distinction between salaried officers and employees on the one hand, and wage earners on the other. Wage earners were defined as skilled and unskilled workers of all classes, including piece-workers employed at the plant, and foremen and overseers in minor positions who perform work similar to that done by the employees under their supervision. The average was computed in the same manner as previous censuses.[18]

The Census of 1940 defined wage earners as those who perform manual work, using tools, operating machines, handling materials and products, and caring for the plant and its equipment. They comprise both time and piece workers. Working foremen and "gang and straw bosses" are treated as wage earners, but foremen whose duties are primarily supervisory are classified as salaried employees. Averaging was done in the manner used in previous censuses.[19]

Manufacturing: The Census of 1900 and earlier censuses included establishments engaged in the neighborhood, household, and hand industries. The number of establishments canvassed was therefore relatively far greater at these earlier censuses than at the censuses following 1900, but as the establishments in the neighborhood, household, and hand industries are for the most part small, the other criteria show less change. For comparative purposes the statistics for 1899 (but not 1900) have been revised by the Bureau of the Census so as to exclude these neighborhood, household, and hand industries. The censuses of 1909 and 1910 and later years were confined to manufacturing establishments conducted under what is known as the factory system, exclusive of the so-called neighborhood, household, and hand industries.[20]

Manufacturing is currently defined as the mechanical or chemical transformation of inorganic or organic substances into new products. The assembly of component parts of products is also considered to be manufacturing if the resulting product is neither a structure nor other fixed improvement. These activities are usually carried on in

---

14. Bureau of the Census. *Fourteenth Census of the United States: 1920,* Vol. IX, p. 17.
15. Bureau of the Census. *Twelfth Census of the U.S.: 1900,* Vol. VIII, Pt. II, p. viii.
16. *Thirteenth Census of the U.S.: 1910,* Vol. VIII, p. 237.

17. Bureau of Census. *Fourteenth Census of the U.S.: 1920,* Vol. IX, p. 16.
18. Bureau of Census. *Fifteenth Census of the U.S.: 1930,* Manufactures 1929, Vol. I, p. 5.
19. Bureau of Census. *Sixteenth Census of the U.S.: 1940,* Manufactures 1939, Vol. I, p. 4.
20. Bureau of Census. *Thirteenth Census of the U.S.: 1910,* Vol. VIII, p. 19.

plants, factories, or mills, which characteristically use power-driven machines and materials-handling equipment.

Manufacturing production is usually carried on for the wholesale market, for transfer to other plants of the same company, or to the order of industrial users rather than for direct sales to the household consumer. However, some manufacturers (e.g., baking, milk bottling, etc.) sell chiefly at retail to household consumers through the mail, through house-to-house routes, or through salesmen. Some activities of a service nature (enameling, binding, plate making, etc.) are included in manufacturing when they are performed primarily for the trade; but they are considered nonmanufacturing when they are performed primarily to the order of the household consumer. On the other hand, some manufacturing industries include business firms which do not undertake physical production but perform only the entrepreneurial function of buying the materials, designing, and marketing the product, and have the actual production done on contract (e.g., apparel jobbers).

Other related and diverse supporting activities are likewise included in the definition of manufacturing and are described in greater detail in the current Bureau of Census reports.[21]

General Statistics for Manufacturing Establishments

Establishments: The Census of Manufactures is conducted on an establishment basis. That is, a company operating establishments at more than one location is required to submit a report for each location; also a company engaged in distinctly different lines of activity at one location is required to submit separate reports if the plan records permit such a separation and if the activities are substantial in size.

Census tabulations of establishment reports, therefore, differ substantially from those prepared on a company basis, i.e., from consolidated reports which combine various types of activities at different locations (thereby yielding a net sales figure for the industry exclusive of interplant transfers but making meaningful geographic tabulations of employment and value added impossible). These consolidated reports also include nonmanufacturing activities of companies primarily engaged in manufacturing.

From 1947 through 1963 reports from manufacturing establishments have been required from all establishments employing one or more persons at any time during the census year.

In the 1939 and earlier censuses, establishments with less than $5,000 value of products were excluded. The change in the minimum size limit in 1947 has not appreciably affected the historical comparability of earlier census figures except for data on number of establishments for a few industries.[22]

All Employees: The category "all employees" comprises all full-time and part-time employees on the payrolls of operating manufacturing establishments who worked or received pay for any part of the pay period which included the 12th and ended nearest the 15th of the months specified on the report forms. At the all-industry level, the employees of central administrative offices and auxiliaries are included. Included are all persons on paid sick leave, paid holidays, and paid vacations during these pay periods. Excluded are members of the Armed Forces and pensioners carried on the active rolls but not working during the period. Officers of corporations are included as employees; proprietors and partners of unincorporated firms, however, are excluded from the total.

Employment and payroll total for central administrative offices and auxiliaries are included in the statistics shown for the years 1954 to 1963. Prior to 1954, this information was not available. The "number of establishments with 20 or more employees" total for 1958 and all previous years and "total number of establishments" total for 1954 and previous years does not include data for central administrative offices and auxiliaries.[23]

Production and Related Workers: This category comprises workers (up through the working foreman level) engaged in fabricating,

---

21. Bureau of Census. *Census of Manufactures: 1963,* Vol. I, pp. 5-9; Bureau of Census, *Census of Manufacturing: 1972,* Area Series, MC72(3), pp. iv-v and Appendix A.

22. Bureau of Census. *Census of Manufactures: 1963,* Vol. I, Summary and Subject Statistics, p. 7.

23. Bureau of Census. *Census of Manufactures: 1963,* Vol. I, Summary and Subject Statistics, pp. 16, 102.

processing, assembling, inspection, receiving, storage, handling, packing, warehousing, shipping (but not delivering), maintenance, repair, janitorial, watchman services, product development, auxiliary production for plant's own use (e.g., power plant), record keeping, and other services closely associated with these production operations at the establishment covered by the report. Supervisory employees above the working foreman level are excluded from this category.[24]

Man-hours: This total consists of all plant man-hours of production and related workers as defined above. It represents all man-hours worked or paid for at the plant including actual overtime hours (not straight-time equivalent hours). It excludes hours paid for vacations, holidays, or sick-leave, when the employee was not at the plant. Where employees elected to work during the vacation period, only actual hours worked by such employees were reported.

Man-hours were generally well reported except in some industries, such as apparel, where work is commonly performed on a piece-rate basis. However, man-hours were not collected for the very small establishments. Man-hours were estimated for these small establishments as well as for other non-reporters. Because estimating was largely confined to small establishments, there is no significant qualification to the validity of overall geographic area totals for man-hours, except for sawmills and a few other industries characterized by small establishments.[25]

Value added by manufacture, adjusted: Value added by manufacture is derived by subtracting the total cost of materials (including materials, supplies, fuel, electric energy, cost of resales and miscellaneous receipts) from the value of shipments (including resales) and other receipts and adjusting the resulting amount by the net change in finished products and work-in-process inventories between the beginning and end of the year.[26]

Capital Expenditures: This category includes expenditures made during the year for permanent additions and major alterations to plants as well as new machinery and equipment purchases, that were chargeable to fixed asset accounts of manufacturing establishments and were of a type for which depreciation accounts are ordinarily maintained. Expenditures for machinery and equipment include those made for replacement purposes, as well as for additions to plant capacity. Excluded from such expenditure total are costs of maintenance and repairs charged as current operating expense; new facilities and equipment leased from non-manufacturing concerns, new facilities owned by the Federal Government but operated under contract by private companies, and plant and equipment furnished to the manufacturer by communities and organizations.

For the years of 1958 to 1963, "capital expenditures" includes expenditures for plants under construction but not in operation in addition to expenditures at operating manufacturing establishments. Prior to 1958, the data represents expenditures at operating manufacturing establishments only.[27]

Dates of Censuses

Population:

1930-1970	April 1
1920	January 1
1910	April 15
1830-1900	June 1
1790-1820	1st Monday in August[28]

Agriculture:

1959	October 7, 1959-Nov. 18, 1959
1930-50	April 1
1920	January 1
1910	April 15
1840-1900	June 1[29]

24. *Ibid.,* p. 16.
25. *Ibid.,* p. 17.
26. *Ibid.,* p. 22.

27. Bureau of Census. *Census of Manufactures: 1963,* Vol. I, Summary and Subject Statistics, p. 102.
28. Bureau of Census. *Census of Population: 1960,* Vol. 1, pt. A, p. vi.
29. Bureau of Census. *Census of Agriculture: 1959,* Vol. II, General Report, Statistics by Subjects, pp. 58-64.